Praise for *Special & Odd*:

The casual reader will find this story extraordinary and unique; as an adopted child I found it eerily familiar. The all too recognisable feelings and fears that Mulholland evokes, make it at times painful to read but never less than utterly compelling. We are all special and we are all odd and this book is a wonderfully insightful exploration – for all of us. *Nicky Campbell, broadcaster and author of 'Blue-eyed Son'*

James Mulholland has a novelist's eye for detail and the complexities of human behaviour and he writes with great humour and honesty. His is a fascinating story, winningly told. *Andrew Cowan, award-winning author of 'Pig' and other novels*

A story told with eloquence, honesty and great psychological reflection . . . the book works superbly well as a story, an autobiography and a psychological journey that would be of interest to other people who are adopted as well as their parents. *David Howe, Professor of Social Work, University of East Anglia, Norwich*

Special & odd

James Mulholland

Published by
British Association for Adoption & Fostering
(BAAF)
Saffron House
6–10 Kirby Street
London EC1N 8TS
www.baaf.org.uk

Charity registration 275689
© J Mulholland 2007

British Library Cataloguing in Publication Data
A catalogue record for this book is available from
the British Library

ISBN 9781905664177

Project management by Miranda Davies, BAAF
Cover photos courtesy of www.flickr.com;
boy posed by model
Designed by Andrew Haig & Associates
Typeset by Fravashi Aga
Printed in Great Britain by T J International

BAAF is the leading UK-wide membership
organisation for all those concerned with adoption,
fostering and child care issues.

Contents

Acknowledgements

Thank you to my parents for their continued love and support; and to Andrew Samuels. I am very grateful to Shaila Shah for believing in the book and to Miranda Davies for her editing, insight and enthusiasm.

About the author

James Mulholland lives with his wife in London. After pursuing a career in journalism, he became a teacher. He has completed an MA in Creative Writing at the University of East Anglia, during which he wrote his second novel. *Special & Odd* is his first published book.

Note

The names of people, places and institutions in this true story have been changed, where appropriate, to protect the privacy of those involved.

For my wife

'Much will be gained if we succeed in transforming your hysterical misery into common unhappiness.'

Sigmund Freud *Studies in Hysteria* (1895)

1

Hope

Growing up, I rarely gave being adopted much thought. That could be interpreted two ways: either my mind did a good job in avoiding a painful subject, or I wasn't much bothered about something that appeared to play no part in my life.

I didn't come across as a troubled child. I always had a best friend, played lots of sport and attained mostly Bs and Cs in exams. There was nothing to suggest that the word *adopted* – which was all it seemed to amount to, a word – could be like a virus, infecting every aspect of how I saw myself. I grew up knowing I was different from my sister – I was adopted, but what did that mean?

On the advice of the adoption association, my parents had told me I was 'specially chosen'. So if it was something to be pleased about, why didn't we go around telling everyone? Why was it something we only ever discussed, or alluded to, when my parents were tucking me up in bed? Clearly, being adopted went in the "bad" column of things about me. But it wasn't like being really skinny, like Danny Holt at my elementary school. It wasn't something people could see. So why fret about it? What was there to fret *about*?

I was in my mid-twenties when I acquired my original birth record and adoption papers from the General Register Office, via a statutory meeting with a social worker. Looking back, I'm surprised I waited so long. Perhaps going out with friends had until then seemed more important; perhaps I hadn't felt entitled, or ready. Back home I breathlessly scanned doctors' reports, court certificates and private letters, gaining a blotchy picture of my biological parents and the circumstances of my birth.

The file confirmed I had been born out of wedlock. Even though I knew it wasn't such a big deal today as in the 1960s, I still felt a flush of shame. Being a bastard was a symbol of the dirt that I had brought into my adoptive family. The word *illegitimate* – written on the application form for the National Children Adoption Association – seemed to encapsulate the difference between my sister, the natural child of my parents, and me.

Other facts about my biological parents more or less confirmed the little information that Dad and Mummy had known and passed on to me. My biological mother had been training to be a teacher when she'd met my biological father, a 'Naval officer lecturing in Physical Education'. There were fourteen documents in all, each laden with between-the-lines information about the context of my birth and adoption. But there was only so much you could take in at one time.

I can remember sliding the evidence of my origins back into the brown envelope and remaining seated on my bed, staring blankly. Where was the scandal, the drama that befitted twenty years of secrecy? On the other hand, would I really have wanted to be the product of an exotic coupling – Picasso and a Parisian dancer? Above all I was disappointed. The mythology had gone, leaving behind my smallness.

The contents of the brown envelope remained undisturbed for the next few years, until I moved to

Cornwall to attend a journalism course. I'd applied to colleges all over the country and Cornwall College had been the only centre to offer me a place. I made sure I packed the brown envelope, however, knowing I would be staying not far from where my biological mother, Alison Prowse, had lived while carrying me.

* * *

It didn't take me long to find Treven Bay, the place at the head of letters sent by Alison to the adoption association. My first Saturday in Cornwall, I set off after breakfast through winding lanes lined with hedgerows. I can still see a band of sea suddenly appearing at the top of a hill, sun sparkling off its surface. I hadn't passed another car in at least ten minutes and it felt as if I were being given a personal welcome, a round of applause for coming even this far.

An old lady was standing a little way down the slope at a fork in the road. I slowed and asked her directions to Kensa Hotel, Alison's home during the pregnancy.

'It isn't the Kensa anymore,' the old lady said. She had a dog, a ski pole for a walking stick and didn't sound very Cornish. 'It isn't much of anything anymore.'

I had stuck a post-it note on the dashboard and remember glancing at it to check I'd said the right name. The old lady leant an elbow on the windowsill and had a read too. My plan of keeping my preliminary search low-key had lasted all of two seconds.

I can hear her next words as if she were standing in front of me now: 'I knew Alison Prowse.'

She knew Alison Prowse! Most important was to stay calm and not cause her to clam up. 'Is the, er, hotel near here?'

She pointed down a lane that disappeared round a sharp bend.

'Did you know it when it was a – functioning hotel?' I asked her.

3

'Mrs Prowse, Alison's mother, ran it for many years.'

I'd not even arrived in Treven Bay and I'd already met someone that not only knew Alison but the whole Prowse clan. It was as if this were "meant". Before I could stop myself I was telling her, 'I'm doing a journalism course at Cornwall College and I'm investigating . . . doing a piece on how Treven Bay has changed over the years.'

I waited for Mrs Williams – that was her name – to straighten up, then asked if I could give her a lift anywhere. She looked at me with placid eyes and walked around the front of the car. I opened the door and waited as she precisely folded herself into the passenger seat, followed by ski pole and dog.

'Can you keep a secret?' I asked her as we set off at a crawl towards Treven Bay and the mysterious place that had been Kensa Hotel. I felt I wouldn't get much more out of her without coming clean.

'Go on,' she said.

'Alison Prowse is my . . .' I thought about saying *natural mother*, the term used by the social worker who had handed over my adoption papers. It would make it seem as if I had 'psychologically integrated the adoption trauma' (or some such psychobabble) and would be no threat to Alison; but it didn't sound right, too disloyal to my parents, too flattering to Alison Prowse, so I said, 'biological mother'. It had a satisfying sting to it without compromising accuracy. 'You see,' I went on, imagining myself in a black and white film with a pencil moustache and clipped voice. 'You see, I was adopted at birth' – at birth, I liked that too – 'and I've come here to . . .' (find her might give the impression I was out for revenge) 'search for my roots.' I sighed. 'To find her, I suppose.'

The old lady said something like 'Well I never.'

'She may not have told her new family, if she has one, so I have to proceed with caution.' Those had been the exact words used by the social worker. In her apricot sweatshirt and comfortable shoes, she'd appeared to be offering me motherly advice when really, it had seemed then, she was protecting Alison Prowse at the same time as covering her own back were I to turn nasty at a later date. She was part of the same shadowy network that had organised the adoption in the first place. Intellectually I could concede that everyone involved – biological mother, social services, adoptive parents – had had my best interests at heart. But emotionally, there was a submerged rage bubbling inside me at how my life had been so complacently manipulated, at how I had always felt on some level like an outsider in my own family.

'She did marry but I can't recall . . . She was a keen surfer.' I remember noticing Mrs Williams had a tic which made it seem as if she were sucking a boiled sweet, and then thinking that maybe she *was* sucking a boiled sweet. From that moment she ceased being a purveyor of destiny and became an old biddy I had to get information out of. 'A big girl,' she said, 'but agile. I can remember her running up to me on the beach, just down there . . .'

I didn't dare stop the car as we were on a bend so I made several glances to my left. A path presumably leading down to the sea was cut into spiky thicket. Coming into view below us was a crescent of white sand with, at the far end, a huddle of grey slate roofs pressed up to the beach: the village of Treven Bay.

Big but agile – as in tennis player, or shot-putter? I wondered. I asked her if it were the beach ahead where they'd met, to slow the conversation down and give me time to absorb this unexpected information, this latest release of physiognomic data on my gene pool.

'I remember her running up to me,' Mrs Williams said, 'and crying, "I'm not Alison Prowse anymore, Mrs Williams. I'm Alison . . ." I can't for the life of me remember the name of the man she married. They run a pub together. Adams. Alison Prowse married Davy Adams.'

I'd always imagined Alison to be petite, all that pacing up and down school corridors. Now, for the first time, I pictured her with a face. And smiling optimistically back at me was Gwyneth, the mumsy therapist I had sought a few years earlier to help recover from being mugged. In the place of school mistress tweed and a bun, I now pictured Gwyneth's soft features and snappy trouser suit. I realised I wasn't surprised to see her standing in for Alison. In fact, it was comforting – Gwyneth was intelligent and caring – as well as intriguing to see what my unconscious had been up to.

I thought back to my three months with Gwyneth, conducted in her tasteful period cottage in Kew. The sessions, as I recalled, had been characterised by my belief that once I'd come to terms with the mugging I really couldn't justify using up any more of her time, and her insistence that I had other issues I might benefit from discussing. No doubt she had had adoption in mind. But as I'd already told her, I never thought about being adopted so how could it be important? Looking back, I can see that the importance I have given to being adopted follows a clear trajectory. Until my mid-twenties, I considered it to have had almost no effect on me; for the next ten years it seemed to have single-handedly formed my identity; only recently have I begun to view being adopted as one out of many experiences that could lead a person to feel alienated. There are probably more people who feel they don't fit in than those who feel they do.

In the end, I stopped seeing Gwyneth because I was constantly thinking about kissing her and felt it made a mockery of the therapy. It never occurred to me that I could tell her about my fantasy, that it would have made excellent therapy-fodder. We parted cordially, with my 'I'm fine' identity intact.

I couldn't think of a way to ask Mrs Williams what she meant by 'big' without sounding vulgar, so I asked her the next most pressing question. 'You don't know the name of the pub, do you?'

'It's not far from here, I know that,' she said. 'I might' (click, click of boiled sweet against dentures/oral tic), 'be able to find out.'

I didn't say anything. I didn't want to commit myself to another meeting or phone call before I'd had time to take in what I'd heard so far. After all, I'd only come here to have a look at the place at the head of Alison Prowse's letters. This was no more my home than anywhere else my adoptive parents might have chosen to live. Coming from the bland commuter belt, I was particularly suspicious of south-easterners claiming Yorkshire, Scottish or Cornish blood. Blood was red and sticky, it seemed to me, upbringing was what shaped your identity.

So Alison and Davy Adams ran a pub near here. How difficult could she be to find now?

'There's the hotel.'

I followed her gaze to three storeys of white-painted concrete wedged into the side of the slope above the lane. The rounded corners and smooth relief made it look like a jelly. Nothing could have been more at odds with the surrounding green hills, sparkling blue sea and restored stone farmhouses. I'd stopped the car and we gazed at the Art Deco-inspired monstrosity in silence. I had imagined, staring at Alison Prowse's letters, an old-world guesthouse on a cobbled street leading down to an esplanade, Mr Softy ice-cream coiling into cornets, strip of sand, then cold green sea. Eventually I said, 'It's fallen into disrepair, looks like.'

'The children sold the hotel after their mother – your grandmother – passed over, must be fifteen years now.'

Biological grandmother, I felt like correcting her. The wording seemed to be growing in importance, taking on the function of a sluice gate with which to restrict the flow of my feelings to a manageable stream.

'It was very much a family hotel,' Mrs Williams was saying. 'Mrs Prowse, your grandmother, would serve the alcoholic drinks herself from a trolley that she wheeled around the dining room.' She smiled to herself. 'Two sherries were quite sufficient for any guest.' We both laughed at the ironic portrait that sounded like it was drawn from fondness, even admiration.

I asked what else she remembered about Alison, as we continued down the lane.

'She was always laughing. She was a lovely girl.'

Her choice of words reminded me of the final paragraph in a report penned by someone at the adoption association: 'The baby was her colouring, fair hair and a pink and white complexion, a lovely child.' A few years on I could have retched on all that loveliness, but right then I still found it pleasing to recall. Alison, perhaps because she was so abstract, had all but escaped my resentment. If I wanted someone to blame for feeling like an outsider in my own family, my parents were nearer at hand.

'How long ago did she marry?' I wanted to know how soon after having me she'd found connubial contentment with Davy Adams.

Mrs Williams replied that, hard as it was to believe, it must have been over twenty years ago now.

I knew from the papers that Alison had been 23 when I was born so she must have been around 27 when she married, young enough for me to have biological brothers and sisters. My sister Rachel, whom my mother gave birth to ten months after adopting me, was fiercely protective of her relationship with my parents. I couldn't imagine her waiting at Paddington Station to welcome any late arrivals to the family unit.

Mrs Williams, switching smoothly to mind-reader mode, was telling me that she didn't think Alison and Davy had any children.

'All the lonely people, where do they all come from?'

That haunting line from the Beatles song 'Eleanor Rigby' summed up how I liked to think of Alison. It was even released the year I was born, 1966, the summer – appropriately – before the hippies' legendary Summer of Love. Maybe she was waiting at the window a few miles from here, at this very moment, for that 8lb 3oz boy with fair hair and a pink and white complexion to return into her arms, transformed into a dashing cub reporter.

I secretly liked to think of my parents as somehow stealing me rather than Alison giving me away. No doubt casting my parents as the villains of the piece enabled me to avoid the more painful reality, that my biological mother had rejected me. Going to the trouble of stealing me also meant that I must be valuable. Lastly there was the matter of convenience. I had to aim my resentment, my frustration at feeling both special and odd, at someone. My parents made the obvious target in Alison's absence.

After dropping Mrs Williams at the gate of a small development of brick bungalows, I retraced to the hotel car park, found a space between the potholes and discarded bottles, and walked up some concrete steps to the second floor, where a balcony ran along the length of the sea-view frontage. The edge was protected by a rail with a wire mesh wall that, in a time when guests had existed, must have prevented them from falling onto other guests on the terrace below.

The view was clearly the reason why the hotel had been sited here. Cliffs reached into the dark blue sea at either side of the bay like crab claws, and in between, the curve of the horizon was interrupted only by three motionless black specks, probably tankers. I stood quite still as a peaceful sensation rose through me. I crossed the balcony and leant on the rail. White paint curled up, away from the wood. I picked at it like a scab. This feels right, I thought. Driving here in the summer for the interview at Cornwall College, windows down, I'd pulled into a lay-by on the top of Bodmin Moor. Something had struck me. I got out and stood by my car. It was the salt air. I watched clouds skim across domes of wiry grassland and told myself it was a good omen for the interview.

Signs, of course, cater to the preoccupations of the interpreter. As I stood on the balcony of Kensa Hotel, recalling the trace of sea air that had wound its way to the top of Bodmin Moor, I felt it could have meant only one thing: Coming Home.

Later, as I write this memoir – how self-important that still sounds – I realise the smell of the sea has meant different things to me at different times. It can recall, together with the rich smell of mud at low tide, the sailing club where I spent summer holidays as a child. Or the North Sands at St Andrews, where my housemate Charles and I would jog to the point, inhaling the wind as we attempted to shake off hangovers from Friday night at the Students' Union. Or Sa Riera beach in the Costa Brava where, after too long in the sun, talking with friends and drinking beer, we would dive into the deliciously cool sea and swim towards the rhinoceros, a rock formation in the shape of a horn far out to sea. But viewed from the hotel balcony, the pure limitless sea meant hope.

The first sign of life I came across was a spider making repairs to a sparse, nicotine-coloured web stretched across a small window. Through it I could see a small painting of a fishing trawler entering a harbour from high seas, surrounded by patterned blue and white wallpaper. The wooden window frame was splitting, algae mapped the grey-white exterior walls. On another side of the hotel, a pool table with balls on it stood at the centre of another rubbish-strewn room, cues leaning against the walls as if I'd interrupted a game between two ghosts.

The hotel's day had certainly passed with the Prowses. But it was easy to picture a time when parents sat on deckchairs on the balcony watching familiar haircuts, towels and swimming-costumes bob in and out of view as their charges followed the snaking path down the cliff to the beach. Decades of laughter and tears, of Daddy twirling his young child like a roundabout, wasp stings and snatched nooky, of sand in everything – all seemed to have been absorbed in the thickets and balcony where I was standing now. For a moment I felt I could hear squeals followed by breathless conversation drift up the path as children rushed to fit in a last swim before tea.

A breeze crept between the buttons of my shirt. I can remember letting the calm feeling run its course, understanding it was out of my control, content to be part of such a wonderful, timeless scene.

* * *

'These cliffs were kindly given to the National Trust by William Thomas Kenver Prowse', read the plaque which Mrs Williams had told me about. So that was why I'd been named Matthew *William* by Alison. One of the screws had come off so the words hung at an angle. I straightened the plaque and thought I might return another time with a Rawlplug and tub of filler. I hoped this wasn't a second, less auspicious sign. For a moment I considered taking, repossessing, the plaque. It belonged to me as much as anyone else, presuming the old man was no longer with us. Maybe I should try to reclaim the cliffs, I thought, only half-jokingly.

'My biological grandfather was a local philanthropist, you know,' I said aloud, liking the sound of that. Listen to you, you actually feel pleased, no relieved, that the father of the woman who gave birth to you and then gave you away was probably posh. I had to admit, if the hotel was a disappointment, these cliffs were a definite reprieve. It wasn't quite a matter of money. I wasn't out here gold-digging – a cliff, I'm rich! It was more a matter of class. Raised between leafy Surrey and boarding schools in

Sussex and the Midlands, I'd been given every chance to succeed. I was well-spoken, had played rugby for the school XV and skied off-piste. I appeared to be like my parents' friends' children. But I had always felt like a confidence trickster, waiting to be exposed. Now with this cliff donated to the National Trust – a benevolence more redolent of the landed gentry than the executive middle class of my parents – maybe I wasn't so secretly common after all. I am aware, of course, how shallow this all sounds.

Before seeing my papers, the only information I'd had about my breeding was a couple of excruciating, blessedly short conversations with my parents. The impression I'd come away with was of a kindly country lass made pregnant by a Navy man, possibly an officer. Then I read my papers from the General Register Office and discovered both my biological parents were university educated. With a munificent grandpop thrown in, that wasn't so different from my adoptive parents: fashion magazine secretary meets partner in a City firm.

William Thomas Kenver Prowse . . . I wondered how the old philanthropist had taken his daughter's unexpected "condition". The application form for the adoption association had been filled in by Alison's hand in blue ink, except for Section 19 – 'A full description of the Case' where someone else had typed:

> *Miss Prowse met the p.f. on the rebound from a broken engagement. Both Miss Prowse and the p.f. were students at the University of Exeter. They had known each other for about one year, I understand there was no serious intention of marriage. Since she has known of her condition of pregnancy she has talked with the p.f. and they both feel that thier [sic] relation is not strong enough for marriage. I have talked over with Miss Prowse the possibility of keeping her baby and I understand that her mother is quite prepared to help her financially if she*

wanted to keep the baby. But Miss Prowse appears to have considered the matter very carefully and is sure in her own mind that the baby should be given the opportunity of parents as soon as possible.

Reading this for the first time, I'd imagined the author to be a Victorian governess speaking in a clipped disapproving voice. P.f. was a mystery; presumed father was my best bet with an outside chance for the pleonastic, and therefore fittingly ironic, paternal father. 'No serious intention of marriage . . . her condition of pregnancy . . . appears to have considered the matter'; that such a judgemental person couldn't spell 'their' only added to the hypocrisy. If I put my anger to one side, however, I could see how revealing this document was in terms of the era, the context in which I was given up for adoption. It was not the Sixties of the Beatles and Rolling Stones, Alison was not shopping at Mary Quant for her weekend wear. It was post-War, bound by shared morals and duty.

A more revealing document in terms of assessing the Prowse family's reaction to the pregnancy was perhaps a letter sent to the adoption association by one of Alison's referees. TW Howarth Esq's answers to the set questions are cursory except on the issue of the applicant's upbringing, where he states, 'Excellent home background with very happy family life'. But before signing off, Mr Howarth adds, 'The event is something of a tragedy to the whole family'.

A tragedy, I wondered, in terms of Alison's heartbreak or in terms of the family name? At no point, I couldn't help noticing, did anyone suggest it was a tragedy for the baby. 'He's moving from a single parent to a married couple with money, how can that be a tragedy?' you could hear them chorus. But putting aside the psychological issue of growing up knowing you are adopted, what if the baby missed his biological mother? He'd been in her womb for nine months after all. Of course one could never prove this scientifically; newborn babies make notoriously difficult interviewees. But it frustrated me the way adoption seemed to be only about satisfying the requirements of both sets of adults.

* * *

A middle-aged couple in hiking gear came springing towards me and I chirped, 'Lovely walk, isn't it?' sounding very much like the cliff was already back in the family.

The couple, who had northern accents, assured me they were having a 'cracking time'. They recommended I follow the path to a 'dolly' cove where an old tin mine had been touched up with polystyrene for use in an episode of the TV detective series *Wycliffe*. We chattered on, about the massive fried breakfasts at their B&B, the Indian summer all this week and a pub, also 'dolly', that they were off to tonight. Unfortunately they were unable to tell me the name of the landlady.

The path was narrow with low thorny undergrowth on both sides, at one point coming to within a yard of the cliff face. I craned my neck towards the edge, glimpsed foamy, slopping sea. Gulls circled and swooped and one little brown bird only flexed its wings enough to stay stationary against the breeze. The bird seemed not to be going anywhere until it had good reason to do so, a worthy strategy, I thought.

The tin mine, a square brick tower with a wooden arm projecting from it, was sited on a terrace cut into the cliff edge. A woman with a dog seemed by her arm gestures to be discussing the mine's architecture with a man in a blue uniform. No camera crew was in evidence, so they had to be part of real life. The man was probably the security guard the northern couple had told me about. The dog, a gangly silver-haired thing, began pulling at its lead as I approached, keen to get to know me better. I slowed in case the woman's grip wasn't as secure as it should be, and overheard her tell the guard, 'I was never allowed to read any of those books, *Poldark* or *Penmarric*, when I was a girl. My mother was a local historian and said they were historically inaccurate.'

I stopped breathing. The file had said Alison's mother was a History graduate. I looked at this woman as she chattered to the guard and as the dog settled back at its mistress' side. Her eyes seemed dark or maybe they were deep-set, her hair wild or maybe just windswept. It was hard to say anything definite about her. But I did feel a brooding presence, even from ten yards away. To avoid being drawn into a conversation with them, I walked towards the cliff edge. I couldn't bear to stand around chattering about a BBC period drama, suspecting what I did. Behind me, that strikingly deep, vibrato voice could be my mother, or it could be someone walking a dog.

I'd imagined standing next to my biological mother in a queue, or being introduced to her as the mother of a new girlfriend, or dragging her out of a car wreck – and somehow knowing who she was. But now that I was faced with someone that could be her, my intuition wasn't as deft as I would have hoped.

'Alison Mary Prowse is worrying because she talks too much,' Mrs Collier JP, from the adoption association, had written in her report, the letters after her name referring, I presumed, to her lofty position within the judiciary. That fitted the woman chattering to the guard about nothing. When would she continue her walk so I could go up to her and . . . say what exactly? 'Hi, Mum.' She'd probably have a heart attack right there on the coast path. I'd have to handle this with delicacy or I could be facing a manslaughter charge.

I could no longer hear the murmur of conversation so I turned to see if they'd parted. The woman was looking my way, while the guard petted her dog. Maybe she'd sensed something when I arrived, or noticed my shifty behaviour and was wondering what it was all about? It would explain her troubled air. She might even know who I was through a maternal sixth sense and be collecting herself for an introduction.

I casually ambled over to the other side of the set, from where I could keep a covert eye on her movements. I traced a finger along the join between polystyrene and real stone but the pounding at my temples obliterated any appreciation of the workmanship involved. According to Mrs Collier, Alison was 'a girl with a perfect English rose colouring, a very strong face', whatever that meant. On the application form, Alison had described her appearance as '5' 7", fair hair, mottled green eyes, pink and white complexion', while her talents and/or hobbies were 'pianoforte, painting, singing, handicrafts, outdoor activities, swimming, riding, walking, music appreciation'. Arty and a bit sporty, then. Certainly that could fit the woman over there, covered by a headscarf and bulky anorak, still listening to the guard. 'Pianoforte' could mean she was either old-fashioned or trying to sound posh.

She seemed to be breaking off from the guard, who began rubbing his hands, possibly in anticipation of the cold evening ahead. 'Come along, Shep,' she said, or something similar, and dog and owner started towards the coast path, watched by the guard. After a moment I followed them at a pace brisk enough to narrow the gap but not too fast to cause alarm. My brain felt like a computer processing a whir of numbers, letters and symbols.

The social worker (who'd seen my papers before showing them to me) had picked out one or two sentences she considered important. I remember her saying she thought 'Miss Prowse says that she hopes to marry and raise a large family, but not with Mr McCleod,' suggested someone with clear life-goals. One document had also revealed that Alison hadn't told her mother about the baby until a fortnight before I was born, which the social worker felt would require great self-control and may indicate a fear of losing social respectability. 'She sounds like Margaret Thatcher,' I'd replied.

But this woman chattering happily with guards had to be more approachable than the Iron Lady. She turned to me, a hand reaching for the dog's collar as I drew level. Close up, her gaze seemed more inquisitive than troubled, although she still seemed sad. This was probably a good thing. If she didn't want to meet me, a familiarity with bad news might equip her to deal with more of the same. On the other hand, I might be about to transform her life.

'I overheard you talking to the guard about your mother being a local historian,' I began. She didn't say anything but I'd got her interest. 'Is that Mrs Prowse?' The words had come to me unplanned, each arriving as I finished the one before, but as I waited for her reply I had to admire the subtlety of my approach.

The lady acknowledged that she was.

We both stopped walking and I looked at her in dumb amazement. The knowing smile made me think she'd been waiting for me to ask that for 29 years. I can remember the inside of my nose stinging, and having to pinch it hard to disperse the sensation. The two of us stood like figures in a fairytale, frozen until one of us said the magic word. Eventually I said, 'Are you Alison Prowse?'

'Alison's my sister.'

Lorna – that was her name – later told me she'd guessed I was one of her sister's errant drama pupils, trying to get something on their teacher. She said even when I told her who I was, it took some time for her to believe me completely.

Looking back on that day, I believe the first thing I felt was disappointment at not being the cause of this woman's pervasive thoughtfulness. That's typical of me, I've got the star role and my first concern is about the support part I've missed out on. Then I can clearly remember feeling relief that my meeting with Alison, were it to happen, would be delayed. There would be time to compose myself. After that my mind was flooded with a hundred interlinked questions, and the difficulty became where and how to begin. It was only that evening, on the phone to my friend Fiona, that I began to realise how literally unbelievable the facts were. You had to hear my voice or see my face to believe them. Even Dickens would not have dared put this in a novel – not all in one day anyway. But happen it did. And as it happened, I simply treated each twist and turn at face value.

Lorna let go of the dog's collar, keeping hold of the lead, and it dropped behind its owner. I'd apparently satisfied one customer. As we continued walking, a thought came to me, *Alison might not have told her sister about me. Lorna might have been too young or have left home by the time the 'tragedy', to use TW Howarth Esq's word, had hit the family.* I didn't want to be like the gay activists who outed prominent people from their closets against their will. Somehow I had to find out how much Lorna knew without letting her guess who I was. Lorna seemed in no hurry to reveal anything, apparently happy to let me continue when I was ready. Eventually I broke the silence, 'Are you the older sibling, may I ask?' You could keep less from an older sister than a younger one.

Lorna confirmed that she was.

'Do you know everything about her?' No one could answer yes to that! 'I mean,' I tried again, 'are you very close?'

'She's my best friend,' Lorna said simply.

'Do you think there's anything major she could have kept from you over the years?'

A current passed across Lorna's face. For the first time she seemed worried rather than mildly entertained by my cryptic questioning.

Out with it, I thought. 'Did you know she had a son?'

Every feature of her face became instantly alert, as if a bell had sounded and every tiny muscle had run to its post. How long ago did Alison have that boy? I imagined her calculating. How old is this man?

I pressed on without waiting for a reply: 'I'm that son.'

'No,' Lorna said. 'I don't believe you.' But her face, which was beginning to light up, said that she did.

'I am,' I said, thinking, 'It's going to be OK.' I could see it in her eyes, heavy now, but twinkling in astonishment.

'Tell me it's not true,' she said, more, it seemed, to herself than to me.

'It's true,' I replied.

Whenever I get to telling this part, I see Trevor Howard and Celia Johnson in *Brief Encounter* seated at a table in a 1940s railway station tearoom, heads inclined towards each other in extra-marital conspiracy. They exchange tight-lipped pleasantries, while Rachmaninov's piano concerto speaks of how they really feel. I find myself drawn to old-style British restraint, even as it chills me.

'It's wonderful,' Lorna/Celia Johnson goes on. 'I can't believe it. Are you really Alison's son?'

I assure her again that I am and feel a big grin break across my face.

* * *

Lorna invited me back for tea. We sat in the tiny cluttered kitchen of her portion of a converted farmhouse. Lorna had grown up here with her elder brother Geoff and younger siblings Alison and John, whose chin I apparently had. In those days the family had owned the entire farmhouse, which was a ten-minute walk from the hotel. When her parents passed away the children were each given a quarter. Lorna's portion had the advantage of a sea view, though by the time we arrived dusk was closing in. Once you knew she was an artist you could see it everywhere: the lightly chipped earthenware cups dangling from hooks under a shelf, the soil-covered vegetables lying in a wicker basket like a still life, an unframed painting leaning against a wall. The overall feel was "shabby genteel". As I sipped the strong tea I felt amazingly relaxed, in no hurry to talk about Alison or me.

Lorna would start telling me something then stop herself, saying she wanted to let Alison tell it. I did learn, however, that all four siblings went to university, Lorna to Oxford, and that Alison was an award-winning chef and touring opera singer. I told Lorna I was chucked out of my prep school choir before I had the chance to sing the solo of 'Once in Royal David's City' – I would have been around 25th in line – for throwing Mars Bars in the back of the van as we returned from a rehearsal at the church. 'It's one of my mother's favourite stories about my schooldays,' I said, hoping Lorna would grasp what I was getting at, which was that Mummy liked the story because it supported her version of me. It showed that they'd given me every chance to succeed, even at such un-Mulholland activities as singing, but there was only so much that upbringing could achieve before genes kicked in and Mars Bars flew and tears were shed. It seemed obvious to me then that the fact I was adopted gave my parents an out-clause whenever I let the side down. After all, if your son turned out to be a serial killer wouldn't it be easier if he were adopted than biological?

In Lorna's thoughtful smile I felt I detected an acknowledgement of what I was saying. But then she said, 'It's like being caught drinking the altar wine. All mums are secretly proud when their son does something rebellious.'

I smiled back, annoyed that she'd taken my mother's side. She seemed to be telling me, 'Not everything is about being adopted, James.' To which I would have replied, 'I never said it was.' But it struck me, with a rising sense of indignation, that everything *was* about being adopted.

Behind every interaction, even with my oldest school friends, lurked the fear of rejection. This led to being hyper-vigilant, which is another word for "chippy". Although I tried never to show it, I could take offence at something you thought before you'd even thought it! It was called being prepared. No one was going to reject me before I'd rejected them. The good news was that the bookkeeper in my head, who was in charge of recording who liked me and who didn't, still had Lorna down as winnable.

I wondered whether to start talking about Officer in Her Britannic Majesty's Navy Don McCleod, to show her, through reverse psychology, how unaffected I was by being adopted. Look how easily I can bring up even its thorniest matters! Alison had written on one of the forms that he was an 'international water-polo player'. But I couldn't think how to introduce him into the conversation without sounding like I was bragging, bragging, in effect, about the quality of the sperm used to create me. How sad would that be?

Instead I let Lorna know I had attended public school followed by St Andrew's University and my sister Rachel, funnily enough, had also gone to Oxford. Christ Church. I told her about summer holidays spent on the south coast racing Mirror dinghies against other children or on "cocktail cruises" with the grown-ups. The latter involved pottering around the beautiful natural harbour in a sturdy wood motorboat – give her a taste of my reportage – accompanied by the low thud of the diesel engine, lapping water and adult laughter that always seemed to come in co-ordinated bursts. When I was old enough I was allowed to sit at the bow, one leg dangling on the port side, the other on the starboard side, hands gripping the rail, riding the swell like a cowboy astride a bucking bronco. We always went with family friends, gin'n'ton and Twiglets for the grown-ups, Coke and crisps for the kids. My mother teasing my father by looking at the lemon wedge at the bottom of her friend's glass and telling him not to be so mean with the drinks. The best part was talking to Daddy about the different classes of dinghy raced in the harbour.

'Look, Daddy: 14s!' We look. I like the way the vertical drop of a 14's bow slices through each wave like a knife. 'Are those Fireflies?'

'They look like Flying 15s,' Daddy says.

'Are you sure they're not Flying Dutchmen?'

'No one really sails Flying Dutchmen anymore.'

'But they're an Olympic class!' I protest.

'Were an Olympic class, James.'

'Are you sure they're not Fireballs?' I know they can't be Fireballs because Fireballs have got a massive red circle on their sails but I love going through the names of all the different classes of dinghy in the harbour that begin with F, which is practically all of them.

'Fireballs have a big red sun on their sails,' Daddy says. 'I think they're Flying 15s.'

'I like Fireballs best.'

'They're good for youngsters starting out,' Daddy says. 'They've got plastic hulls so they're cheaper to run than 14s or Flying 15s.'

Daddy doesn't really like Fireballs. I love them! I love their squared-off bow, the chiselled look of their beam. Also, in a previous conversation, Daddy said Fireball sailors were 'flashy' but I think they're great. They're always laughing and they usually have a girl up on the trapeze, which looks funny. I agree they're not serious like 14 sailors and we don't have any in our club, but, but . . .

'Don't be so mean with the drinks, Adrian,' and our conversation will have to wait. I absolutely love talking to Daddy.

* * *

I was surprised to hear myself recount to Lorna conversations I hadn't thought about in years. Faced with

Alison's award-winning cooking and touring opera singing as well as Lorna's Oxford University and painting, I obviously wanted to strengthen the Mulholland cause. I told Lorna about picnics in the sand dunes at Briar Sands. We'd find a spot away from everyone else, spread out the rugs, unscrew the different bottles for adults and children and tug open bags of crisps. Fortified, the kids would play hide-and-seek in the dunes that undulated like bunkers on a golf course, imagining we were lost in the Sahara desert. Mummy and Auntie Sylvia would watch the boats sail around the harbour, calling us when they saw Daddy's boat appear.

In answer to Lorna's question, I explained that Auntie Sylvia wasn't really my aunt. We'd been brought up to call my parents' friends Uncle and Auntie out of respect for our elders. Lorna nodded, showing she was familiar with the convention. Practically every word you uttered, I realised, revealed something about the kind of person you were and your background. Lorna, whom I didn't think missed much, would be able to give Alison a detailed picture of her biological son as much from my choice of language as from the content of what I said.

I decided to continue the sand dunes anecdote, telling Lorna how we'd keep waving at Daddy's boat – I imagined Lorna thinking of *The Railway Children* – until Daddy and Uncle Harry waved back. Mummy and Auntie Sylvia always sighed that it didn't matter where they were coming in the race; what was important was they were out there on the water. With the daddies waved at, Tupperwares could then be opened, and paper plates and plastic cutlery distributed. My favourite part of the picnic was dusting a hard-boiled egg with salt and slowly biting into the top bit, feeling the rubbery white give and give until snap, the surface broke and your teeth sliced through the soft flesh.

If the Prowses had talent, I was determined to show Lorna that the Mulhollands knew how to have good, clean family fun. I had rarely felt more of a Mulholland than now, under attack from our oldest unspoken rivals the Prowses. I realised what a dangerous game I was playing. What if I wasn't talented enough to be a Prowse and not fun enough to be a Mulholland? At that moment to be a Mulholland trying to have a good time seemed infinitely more secure than hoping to become a Prowse. My parents, I realised, would have experienced a similar anxiety about being Mulhollands as they went through the adoption process, except they were being judged by "busybody" social workers rather than the talented Prowses.

I could remember my mother telling me how Dad booked a space at Harvey Nichols' car park, which was next door to the adoption association, to make sure they wouldn't be late picking me up. My father had taken the day off work and the two of them strapped me into the back seat and drove me home. I imagined my mother turning around to look at me, then turning back and wondering if I was still there. For the next six months the inspector – who happened to be an acquaintance of Dad's – popped round to check I was being treated properly. My parents had been under the spotlight too.

I told Lorna about the mixed emotions and expectations I'd built up from reading my adoption papers. I told her about the description of me as having 'his mother's colouring, fair hair and a pink and white complexion', of being 'a lovely child'. I said it made me happy to think that was how Alison had seen me. I decided Lorna didn't need to know that, soon after the report was written, my mother had had an anxiety fright when finally left alone with me, a crying bundle wrapped in a blanket. She'd bought the cot and clothes but, in my mother's words, 'some things can't be prepared for'. However, that night when she laid me on a sofa next to a friend's baby son 'you gave the competition a thump,' Mummy said, 'and I fell in love with you'.

'Mum became pregnant with my sister Rachel practically the moment she got me,' I told Lorna instead, noticing how forced the word Mum sounded even in front of someone unversed in my family's etymology. In an attempt to jump-start growing up, I had recently graduated from Mummy to Mum (and have since reverted to Mummy as the least contrived of the three options). 'Apparently it happens a lot,' I went on. 'The arrival of the child triggers something in the adoptive mother.'

Lorna said she knew someone to whom exactly that had happened.

'Mum says in her case she believes I made her so happy she relaxed enough to conceive.' My mother's words sounded different when repeated to Lorna, I realised. Lorna, a mother herself, seemed to empathise with my mother, leaving no room for the ironic expressions I would exchange with friends when we quoted our parents at their "best". For the first time I began to see the genuine feelings behind my mother's words, even to take a childlike pride in my part in them.

I found myself wanting to retell everything in this new light. 'Mum had to wear a fur coat to cover the three-month bulge when she went to court to have me legally signed over. She was afraid the judge might not let her keep me if he saw she had a baby coming after all. But the judge simply looked at the papers, looked at Mum and Dad and said, to quote Dad, 'I like what I see. He's yours!'

Lorna laughed, presumably picturing a doddery judge in his chambers peering over a pile of papers at a City slicker in a Saville Row suit and his wife in a fur coat.

'It was April, but apparently a mild day!' I hooted.

As our eyes twinkled in the shared laughter, I wondered if I should be saving all this for Alison. Too late for that now. It was as if I were treating Lorna as a rehearsal, a chance to try out dialogue, tone of voice and expression, before the real event with Alison. I had no feeling I was sitting opposite my biological aunt – a blood relative. The first blood relative I'd ever met! She seemed like an empathetic older woman I happened to have got into a frank conversation with. I hoped meeting Alison wouldn't be this . . . normal.

Lorna, still smiling, refilled our mugs from the beak of a hand-crafted hen tea cosy, without asking if I wanted another. I appreciated the informality. She didn't seem preoccupied with the flip-side of all these anecdotes: Alison's loss. Maybe that would come once the surprise wore off. Or maybe she believed Alison had been better off without me.

'It's ironic,' she said after a not-uncomfortable pause, 'that Alison gave you away and wasn't able to have any more children and your mother, who couldn't have children, had one as soon as she adopted you.'

'I don't think you could invent a better example of irony,' I said, a little put out by her matter-of-fact delivery, which I also found surprising. She was clearly moved when I told her who I was on the coast path; she obviously cared deeply for her sister and had no doubt how happy meeting me would make her. Perhaps she'd comforted Alison over the years and saw no room for regret at this momentous time.

Looking back, I believe Lorna was matter-of-fact because she was thinking about my mother, not Alison. The irony she was referring to was the fact that my mother had tried unsuccessfully to have a child for years and years and then the moment she was given one, she didn't need it any more – not as she had before. The judge's signature making them my legal parents was no longer the most important thing in their life, which it would have been had Mummy not been pregnant with Rachel.

My mother had once said to me, tears welling up in her eyes, 'If you ever want to know how much we love you, if it wasn't for you, we would never have had Rachel.' Now you could take that two ways. From my point of view, it sounded like she was saying I was a conduit, a means to an end. But of course she wasn't saying it from my point of view. What my mother meant was, given the reality that she hadn't given birth to me, what greater compliment could she give me than that I was instrumental in creating Rachel? In this way I was as much a part of the natural family as Mummy or Dad. No prize, however, for guessing which way I'd taken my mother's words back then.

It was the existence of Rachel that gave a physical, breathing meaning to being adopted. When I was too young to understand what giving birth meant, I nonetheless understood that I was 'not like Rachel'. And I knew it to be a negative thing. Why hadn't Rachel been told in hushed tones as she was tucked up in bed that she was "biological"? Being adopted was clearly something you kept quiet about. Within the family we never speculated if I had my biological mother's nose or biological father's sense of humour, whereas Mummy would say Rachel had her father's logical mind or was a stay-at-home like her maternal grandmother. Out in public, my being adopted was never mentioned, to the point where I assumed no one else even knew. My parents' guiding principle was always to treat us equally, which they did. In practice, that meant everyone, including myself, ignoring that I was adopted, in other words pretending that I was a natural child too. (Whoever heard of parents treating a natural child 'as if she were adopted' in order to show how much they loved them?) And hidden inside my parents' entirely honourable guiding principle whirred the engine of doubt, the word "pretend". I had to pretend to be the same as Rachel and all the other children I knew. I had to pretend not to be the person who had got himself adopted. Whatever I had been – and presumably still was deep down – was bad.

Maybe in time, my subconscious game plan went, they'll forget I was ever adopted. The fools! All I had to do was keep pleasing everyone.

The timeline of my adoption was crucial, I realised. Born in August 1966, I spent a week with Alison before being placed in foster care for the statutory three-month window, during which time the biological mother has the right to take back the baby. My parents therefore got me in November, and my mother did not realise she was pregnant with Rachel until February 1967, meaning that we had three months together when I was their only child, and unless they adopted again, the only child they were ever likely to have. So keeping me was far more than insurance against my mother miscarrying. The bond was already too deep to consider giving me back, when in March they met with the judge and I was made their legal son.

Lorna was saying something about Alison being fantastic with Lorna's children. Now that was ironic. 'Especially when I was divorced from their father. You come from a very noble, dignified woman. You couldn't have a finer mother.' She clasped my hands across the kitchen table. 'I mean it.'

Her thumbs were wide and short, the nails thick and cut straight across the top. Hands used to physical work. I squeezed them, then let mine lie in hers until she'd had enough. I'd run out of things to say. I agreed to ring her in a couple of days once she'd talked to Alison, and then I had to stop myself from running to my car, I was so desperate to leave and be alone.

2

Sadness

The secret to being a successful victim is to take who you are more seriously than what you do. Take my first "job" on leaving school. It was the beginning of my year off, as the gap year between school and university was unashamedly called in the 1980s. My father had set me up with unpaid work experience at the City firm from which he had recently retired as chairman. He paid me a living allowance and I stayed in my parents' top-floor London flat, complete with a glittering, 180-degree view of a bend in the Thames.

At the firm, I joined the induction programme for new recruits, all Oxford and Cambridge graduates apart from one tall, blond young man – the son of a friend of the current chairman – and myself. Tellingly, I don't remember being anxious about how well I would perform in such company. No doubt this was partly because, unlike all the other recruits, I was only passing through. But it was also because I was the previous chairman's son, and could imagine I was something special. As I strode into a conference room, watched by a framed black and white photograph of my grandfather, my only concern was whether it was obvious my suit had been bought for me the previous week at Harrods (overpriced and unimaginative) and by my mother (not cool).

After a round of introductory talks, we were told we would be placed in different departments on a carousel basis. I was taken to an empty desk beside Tony Van Dousen, a friend of Dad's whose name I knew but whom I hadn't actually met before. The head of personnel introduced us and, with a smirk in Tony's direction, advised me to 'watch and learn from the best in the business'.

Tony Van Dousen was senior enough not to bother showing me anything he didn't feel like showing me. After a bewildering, high-speed explanation of the 'futures market' and 'hedging', both of which I'd never even heard of before, I was given some ring-binders to have a 'shufti' through. Three precedents were set during my apprenticeship with Tony. Mornings became for reading the paper, set after I opened the financial section of *The Times* on one occasion and then wandered into sport without any reaction from Tony. Afternoons became for sleeping – after I dozed off with equal impunity following a liquid lunch with my mate Richard at Simpson's Tavern. The third precedent, which Tony could have been only vaguely aware of, was that being special and odd, in other words adopted, meant I didn't actually have to do anything. I was an iceberg detached from my ice-sheet, floating around in the sea (to use a metaphor once offered to me by a short-lived acquaintance).

This is not to claim for adopted people exclusive rights to the words "floating" and "detached". Nor are we uniquely placed to be special and odd, a state often described by therapists as 'telling yourself you are better than others to compensate for feeling less than them'. Being adopted merely provides the adoptee with a tangible explanation for feeling insecure. A good friend of mine, who felt he didn't fit in with his family when he was growing up, used to fantasise that he was adopted. Imagine his surprise – and envy – when I finally told him that I was.

Adoptees, I now believe, do not have special insecurities that only we can understand. We only think we do. And in thinking we do, we are able to double everyday insecurities. We tell ourselves we've been left out of this or that because we're adopted. I call this the "doubling rule" because it explains how everyday conflicts and anxieties are "doubled", or blown out of proportion, by the adoptee, who is constantly looking for rejection, taking everything personally.

I wonder if any child growing up feeling marginalised, be it because they are obese, physically disabled or in a single-parent family, would experience the doubling rule to a greater or lesser extent.

Of course, I didn't go around telling myself, *I'm thinking I'm special at this moment in order to compensate for feeling odd*. The whole point of a defence is you don't know you're doing it. It keeps your pride intact. The only person with a problem as far as I was concerned was Tony Van Dousen.

Once the work experience was over, I sneaked on him to Dad, saying he'd shown no interest in me and had left me reading company files for a month. Dad pretended to be annoyed with his friend and with the head of personnel, whom he said had always been 'wet', but I could tell he didn't think it was that important. After all, I was heading off to South America with Richard after Christmas for six months' travelling before going on to university. And after that I had, in Dad's words, 'a lifetime of work ahead', in the light of which, presumably, whatever I failed to achieve in my gap year would pale into insignificance.

What I didn't tell Dad was that underneath my nonchalant appearance I had felt frustrated at being a replica doll in a pin-stripe suit, cluttering his old mate's desk. In fact I didn't realise I was angry at all, let alone that I was angry *with Dad* for letting it happen. I didn't know I *could* be angry with him. Dad was the seemingly effortless family provider, gentle and generous. Mummy, who was the one that set limits and shouted at us when we crossed them, was naturally fair game. But Dad – who was only ever heard complaining about Welsh rugby players, Labour politicians and the French – had always seemed beyond criticism by Rachel and me, though not of course by his wife.

It followed that if I were to be angry with someone, the only person left, other than the impenetrable Mr Van Dousen, was myself. After all, a young man of eighteen had only himself to blame if he failed to make anything of his time at such a prestigious firm. It was preferable therefore to avoid anger of any kind, and instead to pity Richard, working a few streets away as an office boy for a minimum wage and food vouchers. Were Dad and I the only ones not to see that I would have gained far more from rolling up my sleeves and earning my own pay than being foisted on his old firm and given pocket money for turning up?

On leaving university I opted not to settle straight onto a career path. I told Dad that I thought it might be beneficial to gain a little more 'life experience' – his expression – by completing a TEFL course and then spending a year abroad teaching English as a foreign language; in other words have another year off. What happened was I got to Spain and started writing a novel about an ex-public school boy who meets a kooky American girl on a TEFL course in London and they go to Spain together and fall in love.

I was able to shelve the TEFL part of my plan thanks to a trust fund that my father had set up for my sister and me. In my possession was the capital from the recent sale of a house that the trustees, with a nod from Dad, had bought for me to live in while at university. The fund also paid out a monthly income that was just enough for a single person, who didn't need to pay rent, to get by on without working. The financial package was intended as a leg-up or, as my father put it years later, a 'safety net', but was insufficient to support a wife and children with middle-class trappings. The idea was that I would still have to make my own way in the world like anyone else; and Rachel would have to marry sensibly, which was a foregone conclusion.

Even at the time, I sensed that this handout gave a vital boost to my special-and-oddness. Now the oddness in being adopted could be balanced – nourished – by the specialness of my independent wealth. No longer bound by the discipline of necessity, I could give free rein to my feelings of alienation.

I hadn't always wanted to be a writer. The first time I remember enjoying a book was lying on a bean bag, listening to Rachel read aloud one of Enid Blyton's *Secret Seven* stories. It was the one where the seven find a thread of red wool caught on some barbed wire near to the crime scene. Their search eventually takes them to a travelling circus, where they spot a red wool sock with a hole in it hanging on a washing line outside a caravan . . . The first book I read all the way through "for fun" was *Danny the Champion of the World* by Roald Dahl. I read it soon after arriving at boarding school, under my sheets by torchlight, which certainly heightened the drama of the father and son's adventures poaching pheasant deep inside Mr Victor Hazell's silent, guarded woods.

I had a wonderful English teacher at secondary school through whom I got into *Julius Caesar* at O-level and *Macbeth*, *Emma* and *Middlemarch* at A-level. But after *Danny the Champion of the World* I don't think I read another book for fun until my first year at university, when an English undergraduate who lived on my corridor handed me a copy of *The Rachel Papers* by Martin Amis. This was more like it: sex and relationships seen through the eyes of a young man, plus some great one-liners. From there, I discovered the American Brat Pack writers that were big at the time, notably Bret Easton Ellis and Jay McInerney.

I knew I couldn't write like Martin Amis. The plots and characters didn't seem especially sophisticated but his use of language was clearly out of my league. Ellis and McInerney, on the other hand, wrote like people spoke. The power of their novels seemed to lie in their subject matter: spoilt American rich kids who snorted coke, had tons of sex with people with amazing bodies, drove BMWs and didn't work. It was every young man's dream, except perhaps the coke. How hard could it be to do an English version of that? (*Very*, is the short answer.) The story of a spoilt English boy who drinks Bacardi and Cokes, drives a Golf with the front bumper taped up, and has no sex or job . . . until he meets an in-your-face American girl on a TEFL course.

Spain, where Hemingway cut his teeth, had been the perfect place to write my first novel. I'd found myself a ground floor flat in a white-washed building on a cobbled street in old Granada. There was a bar around the corner which served *pan misto* (toasted fresh roll with butter and apricot jam) and *café americano* for breakfast and powerful *ron blanco y cocas* in the evening. The barman, who brushed his goatee against every female cheek that entered the establishment, poured spirits freehand, placing a full bottle of mixer beside the glass. Once, I had to take a sip of neat Bacardi, through the ice and fresh lime, to make room for any Coke at all. I wrote in the morning and then sat in a nearby leafy square in the afternoon, reading other young writers and dreaming of being an *enfant terrible*. I would be giving a reading in New York, sharing a bill with Brett, Jay, Michael (Chabon) and Peter (J. Smith) and girls would be queuing on Fifth Avenue, ostensibly for me to sign their copy of my book but hoping to catch my eye.

Predictably, I got lonely because I wasn't meeting anybody doing the same thing as me. No doubt if I'd taught TEFL I would have found a place within the stream of the city. I told myself anyone could teach TEFL but only a few talented risk-takers became published authors aged 24. I was mining for gold. Maybe, but I was also scared to take part, to try and be a TEFL teacher and make friends and possibly fail. The truth, which I sensed deep down but would never admit to myself, was that I had actually chosen the less risky course, which didn't automatically make it a mistake. The book could have been published, I could have joined the Brat Pack – someone had to. Then it wouldn't have mattered if I'd supported myself through TEFL or a trust fund. But the question remains, would I have chosen writing over TEFL *without a private income*? The answer has to be no, in which case I chose to be a writer because I could, rather than because something inside me drove me to write.

What, though, was so frightening about getting a job as a TEFL teacher and making a few friends in a foreign city? Why did it make trying to write a novel and get it published seem like the easy option? It wasn't my first time away from home, nor did I doubt my intellectual ability to do the job: I had a 2:1 from a leading university as well as a TEFL qualification. In short, I was intelligent and outgoing, so what was the problem? The answer to that is, I believe, at the heart of this narrative.

* * *

The issue of whether I wrote because I could or because I had to gained in importance when I decided to finish my novel back in England. There was no doubt what most people felt the correct answer was: I was a trust fund writer. I can remember the son of a friend of my parents greeting me, 'How's Tolstoy?' Of course I didn't inform him that Tolstoy had been a count with independent wealth. The bottom line was that Tolstoy was published, I wasn't.

I wrote for five years, living off the trust fund income

supplemented by dips into the capital from the sale of my university home. It was a solitary time, staring at a computer all day and eating alone most evenings in one of Chelsea's independent brasseries. Friday or Saturday night I would meet up with a male friend and avoid talking about my (unpublished) writing or talk about it so passionately it became impossible for the friend to refer to it in terms of something as mundane as a job. When I met friends of friends, I never failed to be caught off guard when the inevitable, dreaded question 'So what do you do?' emerged from their mouths. 'Nothing,' I would reply, deadpan, and then cringe as we both laughed awkwardly and wondered where to go from there. If I couldn't bear the thought of that, I would say I was 'writing a book' (never 'a writer', a title reserved for published beings) and then have to describe characters and plot before moving onto an interrogation about agents, publishers and how I supported myself while I was waiting for my big break. All to avoid the humiliating admission, which grew inside me like the voice of a sadistic sergeant major, that I was a trust fund writer, writing because Dad had given me cash in lieu of talent.

The worst part was meeting my patron for lunch. At my mother's instigation, Dad and I would have lunch together now and then at the wonderful Bombay Brasserie in Kensington. Surrounded by palms and obsequious waiters, Dad would ask me about my book. The concern in his eyes was agony. 'I'm on Chapter 6,' I'd say, knowing this would be meaningless to him. Or if I was feeling punchy: 'It's my decision to write, Dad. You don't need to worry about it.' The only thing I didn't say was, 'I'm afraid I won't get published and it will seem like you were right to be worried about me.'

I can see now I wanted it both ways. I wanted to live the alternative life of an artist without the insecurity and eyebrow-raising of parents and friends. I managed, in fact, to pull this off for a whole year by enrolling on a Creative Writing course at the University of East Anglia in Norwich. Those at home were kept happy by it being an MA, while I divided my time between my new American girlfriend, whose way of avoiding getting a job was enrolling on a series of post-graduate programmes paid for by her mother; drinking with fellow hopeful writers; attending book readings; and doing a bit of writing in any time that remained.

But even among my own people, I had to stand out. The Creative Writing group met one afternoon a week. We sat in a circle and discussed three members' submissions, copies of which had been distributed to the rest of us in advance. When it came to my turn, a female member abruptly stood up and walked out. (No doubt she was objecting to the degrading portrayal of a female character in the extract from my second novel, but for what it's worth I would argue the male narrator comes off worse.) Nervous giggles emanated from one or two males as Malcolm Bradbury, the famous writer and course leader, spluttered, 'Um . . . Yes . . . Well . . . Um . . . What do we think of this, um, what appears to be an extract, um, from a novel-in-progress?'

The result of submitting a piece of writing that, irrespective of its dubious quality, must objectively be called hardcore was to alienate Malcolm Bradbury, whose reputation and connections were the main attraction of the course, as well as no doubt more than one graduate member of the group. I believe what I was actually trying to do, however, was establish a place for myself within the circle. Working on the subconscious premise that I was less acceptable than everyone else, I would have to compensate by being doubly acceptable, in other words irreplaceable. I would be the wild one, the Speaker of the Unspeakable. And if anyone rejected me for it, they would surely conclude I didn't give a damn what they or anyone else thought.

Of course I did give a damn but they didn't need to know that. I wanted – want – to be accepted more than anything else. At the end of the course, rather than stay in Norwich while I finished writing my second novel, I returned to London, to the comfort of the known, to my friends, parents, and the dreaded question, 'So what do you do?'

It took six more months of listening to the sergeant major in my head remind me I was an unpublished trust fund writer before I buckled, and enrolled in the journalism course in Cornwall. When it came to a contest between writing and feeling accepted – or acceptable – there was only ever going to be one winner.

Even now, when someone asks me what I do, I flinch inside, then remember, That was ten years ago. 'I'm a teacher,' I say, barely able to stop myself gasping with relief.

As I drove to meet my biological mother I told myself the only thing that mattered this afternoon was that I was not in a rehearsal, observing events, cut off from how I felt, but that I was real, that it would be as much my meeting as Alison's.

*　　*　　*

The farmhouse looked smaller in daylight, an L-shaped grey stone building with a converted barn on the other side of the drive. I parked beside an old black Mercedes saloon and a new mauve people-carrier, wondering which one was Alison's. A people carrier, symbol of New Labour and upwardly mobile young families, did not seem to fit Alison, but you never knew.

I'd expected her to come to the front door to greet me but no one appeared as I scrunched across the pebble drive. The door was ajar, and I peered into the dimly lit kitchen that I'd sat in with Lorna two days earlier. Lorna had said on the phone that she'd suggested her place as a good neutral venue for Alison and I to meet and Alison had immediately agreed. There was a bell, but in the end I decided to call, 'Hello.'

'I'm in here,' a woman's voice called back.

An awful thought stuck me: maybe she's severely disabled? But surely Lorna would have warned me, if only to spare her sister's embarrassment. 'I'm coming through,' I called, my voice sounding remarkably steady. The kitchen had been tidied since my last visit. I'd been to the bathroom but not through the other door, leading to the rest of Lorna's part of the farmhouse. I leant on the kitchen counter, felt my heart pound in my chest. Now I knew how the winning boy on *Blind Date* felt, walking around the stage partition to meet the girl who had chosen him. I seriously considered creeping back to my car and escaping, wheels spinning on the pebble drive. I took a breath and walked through the doorway.

It was like looking down the wrong end of a telescope. Everything in the room seemed to cling to the sides of my vision except the armchair at the far end, which appeared to engulf its occupant. I could make out a loose black dress, black hair, black shoes, a string of white pearls. For a moment we remained frozen in our poses, then she slowly rose, stretching out her arms like wings and smiling openly, her eyes wide, as I crossed the patterned rug that had seen better days. The old lady I'd met at the crossroads, Mrs Williams, had been right: Alison was big but agile. (Later in the evening Alison confessed that she'd worn black and stayed seated when I arrived in an attempt to disguise her weight.) I tried to decide how I wanted to greet her, rather than let her choose: a kiss on the cheek would be nonchalant; on both cheeks a bit more sophisticated, or naff, it was hard to say; a handshake would be very formal; and no contact, rather cautious. Or we could simply hug, briefly, in recognition that this was a reunion. Under the circumstances, any of the above would be acceptable, but I decided to go for the single kiss.

She clasped my hands in hers and we stood staring at each other, our arms enclosing a circle of space, like folk dancers waiting for the music to begin. It was a close variation on the posture Lorna had positioned me in when I introduced myself to her on the coast path, and I wondered if it were a Prowse custom that I'd been spared by the adoption. Clearly I could debate in my own mind how I wanted to greet her, but Alison would be deciding how it was actually done. I stared for as long as I thought I could at her hair, which was raked back from her face by a black velvet-covered headband of the sort, if not colour, I associated with teenage girls, then I looked down at her face, round and expectant. For a moment I wished she were Lorna, whom I'd already got to know and liked. I realised that for the two days I'd been imagining I would be meeting Lorna's twin. Lorna had been naturally maternal – she had children and grandchildren of her own, after all – whereas Alison didn't appear to be putting herself second or keeping herself strong for my benefit. The intensity of her grip suggested I would be the one looking after her tonight.

We had the same arching eyebrows bordered by a tracery of finer hairs. Alison's eyes, which I managed to look into for a brief moment, were brown, not blue like mine, but otherwise their deep-set position and long downy lashes reminded me of a Labrador dog and confirmed that I had found the right person. Alison pulled me into a hug, which I returned stiffly, feeling like a marionette. I gazed at the table in the corner of the room without taking in any of the details. All I could think about was what would my mother say if she could see me now. I almost felt as if she were watching us, or at the very least could sense I was up to no good. 'What made you think you could get away with something as dishonest, as hurtful to your father and me, without us finding out?' I could hear her saying.

A question that had never been far from my mind since agreeing to meet Alison, returned now: What would they actually do if they found out I'd met Alison? Was it really possible they could disown me, or was that rampant paranoia, a revelling in self-pity?

I imagined telling a girl, 'I was adopted and then given away by my adoptive parents when they found out...' It should get her attention for two minutes. It would certainly provide me with an excuse every time I failed for the rest of my life.

But things like that or worse did happen every day in the Sunday supplements. During one of our two conversations about my adoption, my parents had told me clear as a bell, 'We hope you'll never try to find them.' Was that hope made from fear of losing me, or was it the thin end of a wedge of betrayal they'd feel? Was I, at this very moment – as I gave Alison a light squeeze to make it seem as if I was into the hug as much as she – taking the first bite out of the forbidden apple, from which no amount of repentance would allow me back into the family? Maybe my parents didn't even know themselves how they would react until they found out.

'I can't believe it's you,' she said, without loosening the hug. It was the first thing either of us had said in what seemed like a long time but immediately I felt some of the tension drain away. I was here, a 29-year-old man meeting his biological mother, which I was entitled to do for myself, irrespective of my parents' feelings on the matter. The reply to that was, *But would I want to find my biological mother if my relationship with my adoptive mother entirely fulfilled me?* And the reply to that was, *Show me a natural son 'entirely fulfilled' by his mother! The only difference is that natural sons don't have the chance to punish their mums by finding an alternative.* Even if it was only in my head, in meeting Alison I was showing Mummy who was boss. Was I really interested in getting to know this middle-aged woman who happened to have carried me for nine months? I could tell from the way her back was vibrating that she was crying.

'I know,' I said softly, 'I can't believe it either.' I waited for a moment longer, then slowly released myself from the hug and looked around for somewhere to sit. 'It's amazing, isn't it?' I pulled the other armchair nearer to hers, angled it so we were at 90 degrees to each other, and we both sat down.

Alison reached inside a shoulder bag that was leaning against her armchair, saying, 'Your father, Adrian, sent this to me when you were two.' She handed me a framed photo: I am astride a red tricycle in the garden of our home at that time, wearing only a pair of navy swimming-trunks. My thighs are like sides of ham, my back is straight and I'm looking directly into the camera, my mouth wide open in childish delight. I vaguely recalled the photo, or one like it, from a family album. 'I've had it by my bed ever since,' Alison was saying. 'Not a day's gone by, I haven't thought of you.' She made a sound that I'd heard from her once or twice before, a quiet, two-syllable giggle that I took to be a nervous laugh.

I looked up from the photo and smiled reassuringly at her before saying the one thing that was on my mind, 'I didn't know my parents knew your address, or even your name. I thought it was all meant to be top secret!' I added with a laugh to try and make her feel less cross-examined.

Alison bent forward and started fishing around in the shoulder bag again. 'Your father noticed my engagement in the paper and wrote to congratulate me. It's a lovely letter. I've got it somewhere. He said you were healthy and much loved and enclosed a photo – that photo. It was the only time I ever heard from him.'

Trust old eagle-eyes to spot Alison's name in the paper! He once told me of the marriage of a prep-school contemporary of mine he remembered from coming to watch me play rugby. I hadn't spoken to, or of, the guy in

17 years and could barely put a face to the name. 'I remember talking to his dad on the touchline,' Dad had said. 'He owns the strawberry farm on the road into Winbourne, so when I read, "The engagement is announced between Toby, son of Mr and Mrs Roy Bartlett, of Winbourne . . ." There can't be too many Toby Bartletts who grew up in Winbourne.' The thing about Dad's stories was they were always full of details, though not always the ones that added drama.

Alison handed me an unmarked envelope and a folded sheet of paper, saying, 'I could never find you, you see. It was always up to you to find me. I wanted you to very much, but I never allowed myself to hope you would.' She smiled and did her nervous giggle. 'That's why I've kept myself so busy ever since, with teaching, my singing and so on, to keep myself . . .' sobs bubbled up in her chest, 'from hoping.' She closed her eyes and a single tear clung to the bottom of each Labrador eyelash, then trickled down her cheeks.

Don't try to stop her crying, I told myself. I reached over and held her hand on the arm of the chair.

'I'm not crying because I'm unhappy, Matthew,' she said. 'James, I mean. The last time I saw you you were Matthew. I'm crying, because . . .' gulp, 'I'm so glad . . .' and she let rip, quietly, her head bowed, chest heaving.

I sat looking at her, returning the squeeze of her hand. I told myself: Let her have her feelings. The trouble was it was hard to know what to do with myself while all this was going on. It was how a bit part must feel stuck on stage while the hero delivers one of his great speeches.

As the sobs eased, she said, 'I'll be fine now. I just needed to let it out. Read the letter. It's been so precious to me all these years. It was so generous of your father to write to me. I know from the letter he must be a very sensitive man. I can tell what a wonderful father he's been to you.' She did her short nervous giggle.

I took the opportunity to let go of her hand and unfolded the sheet of paper. It was Dad's writing, and began, *Dear Miss Prowse, I hope you won't think it in bad taste for me to write to you* . . . He congratulated her on her engagement and told her to open an enclosed envelope if she wished to know more about Matthew. Clever, allowing her to decide for herself if she wanted to be reminded of that episode, especially now she could be planning a family with her future husband. There was no address at the top of the page and the note was unsigned.

Alison was saying, 'Lorna told me "Don't worry, Alison, you'll like James," and she was right.'

I gave her a smile that I hoped she would consider sensitive – the word she used to describe my father – and then pulled two sheets of A5 out of the unmarked envelope. *Dear Alison,* my father had written, *As you can see from the photo of James (as we call him), taken on his second birthday, he's a healthy child and enormously strong. He's very much a man's man and in fact prefers male company.*

I laughed out loud. 'I love it, it's so Dad. Very much a man's man . . . down the pub with the lads aged two!'

Alison let off a huge laugh that got louder as it got higher, gathering strength like a sneeze.

'Now I believe you're an opera singer!' I said, when it was quiet enough to be heard.

And she did it again, louder, higher and longer than the first: 'Ah-ha-ha, ah-ha-ha, ah-ha-ha, ooh, ooh, ooh, ooh, ah-ha-ha . . . Very much a man's man, isn't it wonderful?' she enthused once she'd stopped laughing enough to speak.

Just here, the two of us, I found her laugh endearing, but I wasn't sure how I'd feel about being biologically linked to it in public. I can't remember all that was written in that letter, but one particular line sticks in my memory: *He likes to pull things apart, but usually out of curiosity rather than destructiveness.* Reassuring Alison that she hadn't sired a future menace to society, I thought. Dad had a big heart, putting himself in her shoes like that. The letter was signed, *A happy father – Anon.*

I kept looking at the letter, as if reading it, to give me time to absorb how I was feeling. A happy father; it was so touching. I wondered if he'd sent it against Mummy's wishes or without her knowing. Maybe they'd composed it together and left off my mother's name to avoid seeming to gloat. Coming only from Dad, the letter with its courtly candour could only be taken as well meaning. In a way he was boasting, but in a wonderful way; he was so proud of me he couldn't help but tell everyone, even Alison. I didn't want to cry along with Alison so I put the letter back in the envelope and picked up the photo frame again. 'Apparently I was a terror, running around causing trouble. There's another photo of me about the same time, splashing my sister Rachel and her friend in a paddling pool. They look like they'd rather be left alone.'

Alison laughed, an unremarkable one this time.

I was aware of my eyes grazing the surface of the photo without really seeing what was in it. That was how I always looked at photos of myself as a child. It was the neediness squinting through those eyes that I couldn't bear to look at. Probably, I thought, because I sometimes saw the same little boy looking back at me in the mirror today and didn't much care for it then.

One photo in particular haunted me for this reason. I'm aged eight, sitting in the garden gripping a plastic glass of Coke, looking right into the camera, attempting obediently to smile. In about an hour, after a last meal of spaghetti Bolognese, which I will hardly be able to touch, I am to be driven by Mummy and my godmother, Auntie Belinda, who is taking Daddy's place because he has to be at work, to my new school; which is a boarding school; which means I will be sleeping there at night as well as doing lessons there in the day. My main concern in about three-quarters of an hour will be that my mother has made me put on trousers, which I cannot believe are required. But Mummy will say, looking down at her piece of paper, that it says I should arrive in trousers. After a good deal of protesting, she'll change her mind and say I can wear shorts if I want. But I'll get nervous and put the trousers on anyway. This is all in the future for the boy in the photo with the glass of Coke, but it is tempting to see in those eyes my whole prep school experience to come.

For some reason I started to tell Alison about another photo, this one taken by me on my own Kodak Instamatic. It shows a barbecue lunch with my parents' friends and their families on the garden terrace of our holiday home on the coast, everyone turning to smile at the camera. The men's hair is short and sharply parted, the women's curled like Jackie Kennedy. A yellow salad bowl, green wine bottles, orange salt and pepper grinders, crowd a bright red table cloth. There are empty places where the younger kids have been allowed to get down from the table to play on the grass. I told Alison that it was like looking into a kaleidoscope – very 1970s. But I decided not to say what had only really just struck me, that it was a classic tableau of well-heeled family life and that it was my parents' big shot at happiness. One marriage, one family, one chance to make it right. And in that photo they're high on it, they've succeeded. They've created something from nothing. Unlike the nothing from something, which in terms of a family, Alison had created.

My parents met at the local rugby club where my father was a player and had formed a circle of close friends, and where my mother came to support her boyfriend at the time, Nick Larson, who happened to be captain. 'But it didn't take me long to see him off,' Dad had once stated, according to a friend of mine who had asked him how he'd met his wife.

'I was devastated when Nick ditched me and your father

was very gallant,' was my mother's more widely known version.

Dad's brother had bought four tickets for the first night of *My Fair Lady*, and Dad, who'd had no "serious" girlfriend up to this point, had to bring a date. He asked my mother.

One story from their early married life evokes that mood of creating something from nothing better than any other. Dad, a hay fever sufferer, had been recommended by his doctor to stop playing cricket and take up a water sport instead, where he'd be away from the pollen. He bought an X One Design racing boat and persuaded a rugby friend who had nothing to do in the summer to buy one too and they both joined Winbourne Sailing Club. The two couples would drive down to the south coast early Saturday morning to be ready for the start of the 10.40 race, have lunch at the club, race again in the afternoon or tinker with their boats (the men) and sunbathe (the "girls"), before driving back to Surrey in the evening (they didn't have the house at Winbourne yet). On the way home they'd stop at a lovely oak-beamed pub. The owner always welcomed them with open arms, and his duck à l'orange was delicious and, in my mother's words, 'had seemed the height of sophistication at the time'.

My parents had created a life, which I, aged 29, had not even begun to do. Here I was with this strange woman, looking at photos of myself aged two. No girlfriend, no career (yet), no home, no hobbies, no passions really, just a probing eye ceaselessly searching for slights, hypocrisy or unfairness. It was worth remembering that when I chose to ruminate on how my parents could have handled this or that differently.

'I always wanted to thank your father for his kindness,' Alison was saying, 'but I never thought I'd get the chance.'

I wondered if she was telling me how grateful she was to my father for sending her the package, or if it was a subtle hint that she'd like to meet the man that had sent it one day. She can want to meet him all she wants, I comforted myself. But it's by no means certain she's gonna meet me again, let alone Dad.

I looked at the folded note and the blank Basildon Bond envelope containing the letter, now on the arm of my chair, once on Dad's leather-bound blotter on the desk in his dressing room. He would have had to put both into a larger envelope and send the carefully constructed package to the adoption association to be forwarded to Alison, unless he knew her address as well as her name. I asked Alison if she had the envelope the letter came in.

She reached into her bag and produced a mid-size manila envelope. She must have been reading the letter while waiting for me to arrive, which was why it was out of its envelope. It was the kind of thing I would have done, hoping to glean some last-minute reassurance from a word or phrase. The writing on the manila envelope was my father's, and the name and address read:

Miss A. Prowse,
Kensa Hotel,
Treven Bay,
Cornwall.

* * *

I felt a tentacle of my parents' control reach up through the floorboards, having snaked a path all the way from Surrey, and encircle me. 'I must say,' I said, 'I find it strange the adoption association gave out your name and address. It couldn't have been just your name they gave out, because how would Dad know it was you that was getting married? It could be another Alison Prowse.'

'I don't know how he knew,' she said, sounding distracted, perhaps because of what I was saying, more likely, I thought, because of the agitation I was displaying.

'It does seem one-sided,' I said, calming my voice. 'I

mean, I can understand why you should never have been given their names and address. It had to be final. But I don't see why they needed yours. The only person who should be able to link the two parties should be me.' We'd known each other for half an hour and I was already making speeches.

'Thank goodness you could find me,' Alison replied. 'It's a miracle you did.'

'I agree,' I said. I smiled reassuringly at her but my mind was still on the name and address on the manila envelope. It meant they'd known the identity and whereabouts of my biological mother from the start and had taken it upon themselves never to tell me. I was almost thirty years old! I felt a rush of blood. When would they stop treating me as a child?

My adoption had always been surrounded by secrecy. It was seldom mentioned within the family and never outside of it in my company. Aside from the two jittery conversations with my parents in my mid-twenties – when, so I'd thought, they'd told me all they knew about my biological parents and expressed a hope that I wouldn't try to find them (later contested) – I rarely gave being adopted a thought, let alone talked about it with others. It was a shock, therefore, when my friend from university, Simon, told me that someone who knew my family had confided in him the reason I could be chippy/odd/standoffish [delete as applicable] was because I was adopted. What was more, Simon admitted he'd agreed with the "family friend". I was amazed and appalled. I didn't know either of them knew, let alone people were talking about it, using it as an easy explanation for things they didn't like or didn't understand about me.

When I thought about it though, all my parents' friends must have noticed my mother wasn't pregnant prior to my arrival. They all knew, all their children probably knew too and had been sworn to keep their mouths shut. Everyone would have been talking about my adoption to everyone else except me. For all I knew, Mummy, Dad and Rachel were forever exchanging the briefest of glances, not even needing to utter, 'It's because he's adopted.'

'What are you thinking about?' Alison asked, with a nervous laugh.

'I was remembering how as a child I used to enjoy telling Rachel I wanted to marry her when we were older.' Why I was telling Alison this I didn't know. It'd only happened once that I could remember and I'd hardly thought about it since. 'M . . .' I was going to say 'Mummy and Dad' but decided 'my parents' was kinder. 'My parents had told me I could legitimately marry my sister because we weren't blood relatives.' I left a dramatic pause, then went on, 'As I recall, Rachel looked like she'd rather hold out for an alternative groom.' Alison smiled tightly at this, perhaps unsure where I was going with it. I steered us into clearer waters, saying, 'By eleven or twelve, she already had her eye on the sons of my parents' friends, who were in their twenties!'

Alison did a shorter version of her operatic laugh and I chuckled along. I could picture Rachel with her first boyfriend, Ed, chattering with my parents in the kitchen at Winbourne. She'd met him at the sailing club, where the core of her present-day social circle had formed. Her friends had also met their first boyfriends at the club – or were working on finding him there soon. They would then take the boy to meet their parents, hoping Dad wouldn't be too competitive and Mum wouldn't flirt with him. It was what being a young teenager was about. Rachel had simply been growing up within the containing arms of her parents.

But to me, it had seemed like she was claiming a birthright, one unavailable to me. I could see myself standing at the kitchen sideboard, observing the timeless family scene, my eyelids drooping with envy.

Alison heaved herself out of the armchair, asking me to

excuse her for a moment.

I wondered what she saw when she looked at me. Was it an envious boy-man, or a cub reporter with an exciting future ahead of him? Maybe she saw her baby, dressed up in a 29-year-old body. I knew which the real me was (boy-man), which was the one I wanted to be (cub reporter), and which the one I didn't want to think about (frozen-in-time baby). I can remember feeling as if I were being physically drawn into the armchair by the dead weight of self-pity, and telling myself, Don't give in. Be the cub reporter. Find out the facts; assess them objectively; write a balanced piece. This was how I should treat life if I wanted to move on.

Seen from this viewpoint, it was simply part of the natural course of events that my sister should take her place in the social scene at Winbourne Sailing Club. While my parents had pre-lunch drinks on the club terrace or attended fundraiser dinners, Rachel was carrying out her role as a youthful Mulholland, gossiping with friends on the jetty, snogging boys at discos held in the sail hangar – until she settled on Ed – and going around to friends' homes, whose parents were out, to sample their drinks cabinets.

I, on the other hand, stuck to the company of my oldest friend, Richard. For the first part of the summer holidays we would stay at his home, while we competed in local tennis tournaments, and then the two of us would decamp to the south coast. His mother would drive us down to a halfway point and hand us over to my mother, presumably trying not to punch the air until she could see my mother's car, with us inside, disappear in her rear-view mirror. Safely at Winbourne, Richard and I would spend our time sailing or fishing in Dad's rowing boat, stocked up with ginger beer bottles filled with Whiskey Mac and a packet of Silk Cut. That made us harder than the others, if nothing else.

While Richard and I had been doing our own thing,

observing Winbourne society from a safe distance, Rachel had been growing up within the family, bearing the Mulholland standard into the next generation. Her successes and failures were the family's dramas. I could see now that, as I'd watched my parents chatter with Rachel and Ed in the kitchen, I had felt jealous, of course, that my younger sister was being treated like an adult, jealous that she had a boyfriend and was part of the social scene at the club, but also aware that I was on the outside looking in, and that that was how it had always been.

To this day, whenever I go to stay with my parents in Winbourne, I get butterflies in my stomach as the tyres of my car crunch against the pebbles in the drive. Once I've parked, I sit there for a minute, composing myself. I can't believe I'm 38 and I can still feel like I'm 14. Last time I went down my wife-to-be, who was sitting beside me, asked if anything was wrong. I couldn't exactly say, 'I'm adopted'. Even her patience has limits. So I pulled myself together and said I must be tired from the drive.

When she came back into the room, Alison perched on the arm of the sofa and said that while she was out she'd been wondering what age I'd been when I was told I was adopted. I must have looked cagey because she quickly added that I didn't have to tell her if I didn't want to.

I could hear myself thinking that she was controlling the agenda of the conversation. *It should be you*, the voice said.

Just answer the perfectly reasonable question, replied another voice – the cub reporter?

I told her that my parents had been advised by the adoption association to tell me that I was adopted at the earliest possible moment. This way I could never accuse them of lying to me. It also ensured that I found out from them and not from the child of a friend of my parents.

I said that I didn't actually remember being told for the first time, although the first words I could ever remember saying were to my father as he knelt beside my bed, "tucking me up" for the night. For many nights in a row, I had kept asking him, 'Who do you love more, me or Rachel?'

'We love you the same,' he'd always replied, until one night he said, 'We love you more, but don't tell Rachel.' When I asked him why, he replied, 'Because mummies and daddies always love their oldest child most.'

I told Alison that many years later, when I'd asked him how he came up with that ingenious reply, he said he didn't remember saying it but that if he had, it must have been the only way he could think of to soothe my worries.

Alison was transfixed by the story. Her eyes looked sad, yet I could tell she wanted me to go on. So I said that I imagined it'd been Dad that first told me I was adopted, and that he'd told me as he was tucking me up in bed. I told Alison that I could only remember discussing adoption as something that I already knew about. Probably this was because my comprehension of the word adopted grew gradually as I grew, which was the whole idea of telling me from the moment I started differentiating spoken sounds.

I didn't want to sound too whiny, so I left unsaid that in introducing me to the word at age three or four, there was a good chance I would grow up believing it must be fairly important somehow, which was what happened. I didn't blame my parents for following the advice of the adoption specialists and telling me as early as possible. Who would dare not to, with so much riding on the outcome? But thinking about it now, it was chilling to realise that one of the first things I'd learnt about myself was a complicated, shame-inducing, terrifying word whose meaning I would take years to understand, let alone come to terms with.

There was one more possible explanation for how I grew up already knowing, but I felt it could derail Alison and the evening if I told it to her. It was the possibility that I might have already known because I remembered, on some subterranean emotional level, my biological mother.

Of course that could never be proved, but there was something about the lack of surprise in my early memories of discussing being adopted that suggested it was at least a possibility.

Alison was looking at the photo of me she'd had for the past 27 years. At any rate, I realised with a mixture of relief and regret, here was not the person whose arms I may have been yearning for since last feeling their security, familiarity and rightness aged ten days. That person was as gone forever as the baby who'd grown into the boy-man I was today. It made you wonder what kind of dubious re-enactment we were putting ourselves through at this moment. For some reason I decided to say, 'My parents have always tried to protect me. We never mentioned my being adopted because they wanted me to think of myself as their real son – the same as Rachel.'

I was aware as I said this of a desire to be loyal to my parents and not hold back in praising them, even if it meant upsetting Alison. (I never thought that Alison might be pleased to hear good things about the adoption, assuming instead that she coveted the parental role, that she'd given me up unwillingly and still felt possessive about my upbringing. Perhaps, after all, it was I who was possessive about her.)

Alison smiled into my eyes. 'I think it's remarkable,' leaning forward from her perch on the arm of the sofa and taking hold of my hands, 'remarkable that you came to find me. I'm so happy you've got such wonderful parents – ooh,' she said, letting go of my hands, 'I've got some champagne in the fridge. Would you like some champagne?'

I always connected champagne with having to be cheery and I didn't want to have to be anything tonight. I also connected it with celebrating something and I wasn't sure what she thought that might be. I'd happily drink to our reunion after 29 years but not to more meetings in the future when I hadn't decided if that was what I wanted.

'Would you rather have a cup of tea or coffee?' she said, straightening out the bottom of her dress. 'I doubt Lorna's got any soft drinks in the fridge.'

I reminded myself she could conclude whatever she wanted from us sharing a bottle of champagne. If I didn't want to meet her again, it wouldn't happen. 'Champagne would be great,' I said, deciding to go with the flow.

I watched her thighs brush both sides of the doorframe as she swept into the kitchen. Maybe she thought alcohol would loosen us up and anything but champagne would seem stingy. Maybe she drank it every night! The thought of cool frisky bubbles giving my overactive brain an alcoholic Jacuzzi was certainly appealing.

Alison got me to pop the cork and fill the glasses. I stepped in with the toast, 'To meeting each other again after 29 years'. We clinked glasses and sat back in the armchairs, sipping. I studied the bubbles in my glass as a silence, not unwelcome, followed.

She asked me if I'd received the little quilt she knitted me soon after she gave me away. I said I hadn't and we agreed the adoption association probably had a policy not to forward gifts from biological parents, though I privately wondered if my parents had immediately disposed of it. I sensed us slipping into a fraudulent sentimentality: Alison gave me away, my parents took me in, no amount of champagne or hand-woven quilts would alter that.

I was relieved when she moved on to describing how Lorna broke the news of meeting me. 'She came over for Sunday lunch – yesterday. It seems like weeks ago . . . so much has happened!' Alison laughed. 'We were having a drink before sitting down to eat. My brother John – your uncle! – was there.'

I smiled thinly, waiting for her to go on. John was my biological uncle whether I liked it or not, but I didn't have to acknowledge it until I was ready. The thought of all those aunts and uncles, cousins and nephews and nieces, whom Alison knew intimately and I didn't know at all, made me uneasy. Like the champagne and quilt, I felt she was introducing outside influences into a matter between her and me.

I looked at her as she talked about the 'lovely traditional Sunday roast' she'd prepared for Lorna and John and, of course, her husband Davy, and I couldn't accept I'd spent nine months inside her. Maybe even people who grew up with their biological mother couldn't really accept it, or shied away from the idea. You might be wanting too much too soon, I told myself, if you're hoping to be instantly anchored after 29 years of drifting, just from being in the same room as the woman who gave birth to you.

'Lorna took me to one side,' Alison was saying, 'and said "I met someone really important to you yesterday on Vean Point." I couldn't guess who it was. I thought it might be an opera singer I'd lost touch with. I couldn't believe my ears when Lorna said "I met your son, James." But I knew by her face she was serious.'

'You never guessed it was me?'

'Never. As I say, I've never allowed myself to hope you'd find me. To hope you'd want to find me after what I did to you.' Tears surrounded her eyes. She looked into her lap, sucked her lips into her mouth and turned to me saying, 'What I did was against nature. Not a day's gone by I haven't regretted it.'

There was a noise at the back door, the sound of it being closed, feet wiped. We looked at each other in shocked silence, one might even say guiltily. Alison obviously didn't know who it was either. We were meant to have the place to ourselves for the evening. Lorna was having dinner with her daughter Ann, son-in-law and baby grandson at their home nearby. The person seemed too plodding and noisy to be a burglar.

'Wh-who is it?' Alison called eventually in a reedy voice.

A long face appeared around the doorframe, with a goatee beard, droopy eyelids and a mop of hair, grinned and then disappeared. 'Hi, Alison,' a voice called.

'Lorna's son Thomas,' she said to me, pulling a helpless face. 'Hello there, Thomas,' she called back. 'He must have come down from Manchester,' she explained. 'He's a student there at the university. He can't have told Lorna he was coming,' and she pulled the helpless face again.

Thomas padded into the lounge, woollen socks bagged at the toes, and collapsed his tall, bulky frame backwards onto the sofa opposite us. 'I'm bushed,' he sighed. He rolled onto his side and sat up. 'Sorry, I'm Thomas,' he said to me.

I shook his outstretched hand across the coffee table. 'James,' I returned, deciding two could play it cool. I felt I had more right to be here than him in that this was his aunt's big moment, but I also felt dirty inside compared to his scruffy undergraduate manner, where all the muck was on the outside. I imagined him to be kind and easy-going and clean on the inside, no fiddling around with two mums behind the bushes for this young man. 'Have you just driven all the way from Manchester?' I asked, just one regular bloke talking to another.

'Via Bath,' he turned to Alison, 'where I had to pick up something from Eva to give to Mum,' and he sighed again.

'You poor thing,' Alison cooed in a voice both adoring and mocking.

'Like where are you from, James?' he said, dragging his eyes from the sweating bottle of champagne on the coffee table.

'Her,' I said, pointing sideways and I turned to Alison as we burst out laughing together.

'Ah-ha-ha, ah-ha-ha, ah-ha-ha, ooh, ooh, ooh, ooh, ah-ha-ha,' Alison roared, slapping her knee at the same time. 'Tommy ooh, ooh-ha-ha, Tommy, this is my son James.'

'I better,' he said standing up, 'get a glass to toast you

two,' and he padded into the kitchen.

Most of the time, as I chatted with Alison, I forgot whom I was talking to. Conversation flowed easily once Thomas had left to join Lorna at his sister's. His visit had broken the tension and brought us down to earth.

She told me about the drama classes she was teaching at her old school, which she found 'exhausting' but 'exhilarating', about how busy the pub had been over the summer. I told her about the journalism course: we had four months to pass exams in local and central government, journalism law, and reporting, as well as attain 100 words per minute in shorthand. The other students were mostly my age or younger, recent graduates. The guy I was sharing a house with, Greg, was fresh from Nottingham University and missing his girlfriend. See, I was a normal guy; I could talk about girlfriends and courses and life-size ambitions.

Even when she talked about her sister's generosity in allowing her to take such a part in bringing up her children, or when I described the sense of belonging I had as a boy watching rugby with my father, shadowing his thigh as he strode up and down the touchline; even when sensitive areas such as these came up, I was barely aware of talking to the person that I might have grown up calling "Mum" under different circumstances. She seemed like a woman from an older generation whom I was getting to know for some reason; perhaps we were sitting next to each other on a long coach journey, something like that.

Then it would hit me. I'd look at her and realise this was the woman who more or less created me. I'd wonder if she could connect the person she saw before her with the baby she held in her arms for the first week of his life. For my part, it was reassuring to have confirmed that I came from a real human being rather than a row of beds or some formless female of the imagination. Reassuring, not world-shattering, not even comforting: reassuring. Looking back,

I think even reassuring was overstating it, and confusing would be nearer the mark.

* * *

'We used to go to Seaview in the Isle of Wight when I was a child.'

'One of the family went there,' Alison said. 'I think it was my brother John. He brought back a test-tube filled with different coloured sand in layers.'

The clearest image I have of Alison that night is of her sitting on a bench in the garden of the Shipwright's pub, where we went for some food to soak up the champagne, my turquoise cagoule which I'd lent her pinching at her shoulders and under her arms. It had been a warm day but a late September chill blew from the Helford Estuary below, into the pub garden – a patio with picnic tables. We talked to the sound of lapping water and clinking rigging, the only customers outside. Alison was wearing a thick jumper under the cagoule and every time she leant forward she looked like the Michelin man. She seemed very different from my adoptive mother then, who wouldn't have left the house without sufficient clothing, including a stylish coat.

I think their opposite characters allowed me to forget for much of the time the guilt I felt obliged to feel for two-timing Mummy with Alison. It wouldn't have been so easy if my biological mother had been Lorna, whose London ways in some ways resembled my mother's. 'The different colours of the sand are real, you know. They're not dyed,' I said.

Alison sipped her bitter lemon. Anything more than two glasses of alcohol, she'd told me, and she was liable to get emotional. That, bearing in mind her display so far, I considered to be a warning worth taking seriously. 'It's like those B52 drinks the airbase chappies drink at the pub,' she said. 'Davy has to pour the different colour liqueurs on top of each other without letting them mix. It looks pretty, anyway.'

'Tastes good as well,' I said. See, your boy can have a good time too.

She pulled a sickly face, then, struck by a thought, asked, 'Would you like one? I'll get you one, if you like? Go on.'

I shook my head. 'No.' I'd been brought up to say 'Yes please' or 'No thank you, Mummy or Daddy,' while other children nodded or shook their heads, often without a word. I was determined to be a nodder and a shaker with mother number two from the start.

She passed the test, not seeming to notice my curt response. 'You probably shouldn't as you're driving,' she agreed. 'Carry on telling me about the Isle of Wight, if you like. I talk too much, I know.'

'We used to go there for our summer holiday. Swimming, making sandcastles.' (This was before my parents had bought their holiday home in Winbourne.)

'Priceless, isn't it? That's how we spent our childhood, on the beach at Treven Bay. I'm so thankful you've grown up knowing the sea and family life. I . . . Go on, I mustn't interrupt.'

'There was this café we went to every year, as a special treat,' I said. 'It was bright and clean with wooden tables, and I don't remember it being smoky so I think it must have been No Smoking. Every year I'd have scampi and chips followed by a Knickerbocker Glory. You know what they are?'

'Lovely! Prawn cocktail, steak and Knickerbocker Glory or crème caramel, that's all we ever seemed to sell at our first pub. I hope our food's coming soon, I'm getting desperate.' She sighed heavily. 'I know I need to lose weight, James. It must be an awful shock for you to have found someone so large. Do you mind?'

I shook my head vigorously. 'It's not important to me in

the least.' In fact, in a way I liked it: I came from solid Cornish stock. 'I never had scampi or a Knickerbocker Glory anywhere else,' I went on. 'I could never finish the Knickerbocker Glory. It had tinned fruit in cubes and Walls ice cream, neither of which sound that great nowadays, but they were then.'

Alison sat forward, resting her forearms on the table, her shoulders pushing at the seams of my cagoule, an almost off-puttingly attentive expression on her face. 'How old were you on those holidays?'

'I was born on August 12th 1966 at...' I raised my eyebrows at her, waiting for her to supply the time of day.

'Weybridge.'

I was surprised she got that wrong. 'Woking,' I said.

She pulled an embarrassed face. 'Weybridge, Walton, Woking, it's all Surrey to me!'

The file had said she had me in Woking to be near her brother and sister-in-law who lived in Byfleet. Presumably it meant she'd also be nearer the adoption association in London, and my interim foster mother in Kent. Given what she was undergoing then, she could be forgiven for confusing Woking and Weybridge. She probably could have been in Weymouth or Wolverhampton for all it mattered to her. 'What time of day was I born?'

The question seemed to ruffle her a bit, but it could have been that she was wracking her brains. 'I think,' she replied. 'It seems like a dream. I wanted to put it all behind me, I'm afraid. I remember it was dark all the time in the hospital. The curtains were always shut for some reason. I think it was early morning, before dawn.'

Giving birth in a strange, darkened room miles from family and friends, it sounded like a Soviet era psychological restructuring programme. I thought of my first night at boarding school, lying on a hammock-like mattress, waiting. The sound of another boy turning in his bed was amplified by the silence like a high-powered microphone picking up small animal noises in a nature programme. Then suddenly the door opened and an older boy came in, took off his clothes, folding them on his chair as he went, put on his pyjamas and slid between his sheets, all with barely a rustle. It was quite incredible how humans could bend to the will of other humans without even a murmur.

'I want to say we started going to the Isle of Wight in 1970, when I would have been four, but I think it was a year later,' I said, wanting to move the conversation away from hospitals, birth and death. 'Were you into rock music then?'

She looked perplexed by my apparent change of direction. 'Not really, no. I liked the Beatles. We all did.'

'Jimi Hendrix played his last concert at the Isle of Wight Festival in August 1970. A month later he died from drugs.' How carefully I chose my words, how self-conscious I was. I said 'drugs' rather than 'a drugs overdose' to sound a bit naïve, Cornish, lovable. Next I would be putting a slight lisp in my voice. The problem with all this faux innocence was that if she started to like me – say it, love me – it wouldn't be me she was loving and so it would end up making me feel worse, not better.

'I've heard of him, but I don't know his music. Is it good? You like him, do you?'

'He was a genius,' I said, 'in a genre where the word has long since become meaningless through overuse.' Shut up, James. 'Why I mention it is this young man with long hair and bare feet came into the café once when we were there. If we first started to go to the Isle of Wight in 1971, this was probably '73, when I was seven. It was the first time I'd seen a hippie and the only one I remember from my childhood.' Childhood, not when I was a child. Hear the innocence, the sweetness, in that word, and see what you missed. 'He had girls' hair yet he was obviously a boy. He wasn't wearing shoes in a restaurant, which I think would have shocked a lot of people outside London and the cosmopolitan places, even in 1973.' Culturally sensitive without being politically correct.

She nodded her head solemnly. 'Men only started coming into pubs in Cornwall without shirts on in the 1980s. Before then it was unheard of. I blame Thatcher.'

'Anything goes as long as you've got the money.'

'That's my boy!' she laughed.

I'd voted for John Major, but we didn't want reality to get in the way. I ploughed on, 'The hippie ordered two slices of bread and butter and a cup of tea. I watched him sit there eating his bread and butter and drinking his tea. He was skinny and bread kept getting stuck at his Adam's apple so he had to flush every bite down. I'd had scampi and chips and most of a Knickerbocker Glory and I couldn't understand why he only wanted bread and butter and tea.'

'He probably couldn't afford anything more,' Alison said. 'He was probably a student.'

'Probably,' I said, consciously having to resist getting irritated by her interruptions. Couldn't she tell there was a time for "contributions" and a time for sitting back and allowing a Writer to weave his magic? 'But I remember asking my mother why he was only having bread and butter and tea.'

'What did she say?'

'She told me to stop staring, then whispered, "He looks well fed to me."'

'Why did she say that?' Alison asked.

'I don't know. I just remember Mummy saying it. It made me feel better. I didn't think about what I was eating anymore. I got into Jimi Hendrix,' I went on, 'when I was at university, then I found out he was at the Isle of Wight in 1970.'

Her face lit up. 'Was the hippie Jimi Hendrix?'

I didn't want to tell her about Jimi's demise again so I

decided to explain it in another way. 'Jimi was black, the hippie was white. But finding out about the concert enabled me to contextualise our holidays there.'

She was perplexed again.

'What part don't you understand?' I'd tried to say it conversationally but it still came out like I was calling her stupid.

She didn't seem to clock the insinuation, or chose to ignore it. 'I'm still not sure about the connection between Jimi Hendrix and the café – the different dates. I like the story,' she held my arm. 'I like it. I can see you all in the café.'

'I don't get the connection either,' I said. I'm a writer, you see. And writers don't explain their conceits. 'It's a way to tell you about my childhood.'

She squeezed my arm as a waitress came through the french windows with a tray of food. 'Thank you for telling it to me.'

Alison apologised several times for eating steak, without explaining exactly what was wrong with having it, while I looked down regretfully at my brick of defrosted lasagne and cardboardy tomato wedges. Eating at least provided us with a rest from non-stop talking.

We took coffee at a corner table inside. After we'd opened up creamers and sachets, stirred and sipped, Alison said, 'I expect you want to know about Don and me?'

'Once upon a time there was a...' I said, trying to sound nonchalant, as my heart thudded.

She laughed. 'Don was very handsome and athletic. He played water polo for England. In those days I was much slimmer than I am now. It's working in the kitchen that does it. I'm good all day and then I'll sneak a pudding last thing at night. You don't want to hear about my eating habits!

'Throughout my time at university, in Bristol,' she continued, 'I was in a relationship with a man who loved me very much. This was before I met Don, your father. Ben would have done anything for me. But he was a shy man. We never more than kissed each other in three years. After Bristol I went to stay with Lorna and her husband in Norway, where they were living. Only then did I have the courage to break it off between us, by sending him a letter.'

It was interesting how I'd flinched inside at the mention of Ben never more than kissing her. The description implied that she'd had other plans. I realised how attached I was to the idea of my illegitimate conception being the result of a moment of madness. But there's no need to over-react, the cub reporter in my head told me soothingly. Having desires doesn't make her a slut – just honest.

Alison took a deep breath, staring at her hands. 'The next autumn I went to Exeter University to do a diploma in education and Don was in my year.' She looked up at me. 'I don't want you to think I'm a promiscuous person. I'd never done anything like it before. But that was how it was.' She looked back down at her hands. 'There was no real commitment between us. We got on well. It was a bit of fun, really.' She looked up at me again, smiling weakly.

I returned the smile but didn't say anything. Even though I was relieved to hear her say it, and believed her, I didn't want to let her off so lightly. She could have all the time she needed to incriminate herself, if the whole story was not yet out.

'We went away to our work placements during the spring, so by the time I met Don again, in the summer, I was six months pregnant. When I told him he listened quietly, and asked if I needed any money. I said no.

'My mother was very ill at the time, from a brain haemorrhage, so I was nursing her and running the hotel. My father had died tragically early of coronary thrombosis. He was physically strong as a lion; no one could believe he had a weak heart. Lorna was in Norway with her husband, my older brother was living in Surrey and of course John was a pup. He was very affected by Daddy's death.'

She drew another deep breath, then continued. 'Right up to a week before your birth I was scrubbing dishes and making beds. The only person I told about my pregnancy was Don, no one else knew. I was slimmer in those days so it didn't show.' She spoke like an opera singer, gradually squeezing out each lungful of air down to the last molecule before drawing another. I didn't follow how being slimmer made the pregnancy show less. Surely the same-size bulge would show more on a smaller figure? But I decided now would not be the right moment to question her on this matter, weight clearly being a sensitive subject.

'The University gave me special dispensation to work the summer term from home because of Mummy's illness. I only went into Exeter once or twice the whole term and I think I only saw Don once, to tell him about – you!' She cackled with a forced laughter that sounded like a maraca.

The adoption papers, and now Alison, had said my biological father played water polo for England. I imagined water droplets clinging to the hairs on his buff chest as he stood on the podium waving to fans, one of whom, unbeknownst to him, was Cornish lass Alison Prowse. One of the papers, completed in Alison's hand, also revealed Don was the son of a plumber, had attained a Physics degree at Manchester and 'had a happy home life – his family were very proud of his success'. I wondered how proud they'd have been of his less public achievement. Maybe he'd told them about me, but I didn't think so. The guy tried to pay Alison off, he knew when to excuse himself from the kitchen. Probably scared to death, poor water polo hero.

'That must've been a hellish time for you,' I said. 'It's hard to think what else could have been stacked against you.' I wasn't buttering her up either.

'Somehow I just kept going.' Smiling at something, she went on: 'I didn't tell Mummy until two weeks before you were born. I didn't want to add to her worries. I can't believe how I coped when I think about it now. I was completely alone – except for you.' She laughed nervously. 'You didn't give me any trouble.'

Not then, I felt like saying, but instead I said quietly, 'Maybe I sensed you already had enough on your plate.' Steady on, you're not trying to seduce her.

'I think you did.' She touched my arm, saying in a deliberate tone, 'I think I must've been in shock.'

I remembered a report by someone at the adoption association quoting Alison as saying her mother 'rose to the occasion' on hearing of the pregnancy 'and said if she wanted to keep him she would help her financially', but Alison 'felt it was not fair to keep him, especially as he was a boy'.

On cue, Alison said, 'I'm so glad you've got such a loving, attentive father. One of the main reasons I gave you up for adoption was I saw how much John lost out growing up without a father.'

That and wanting to be unencumbered for when you meet the man you want to marry and have children with, I thought but didn't say. Didn't say. It should be on my tombstone, 'Here lies James Henry Mulholland, who Did Not Say'.

I thought about her vision of my father, which, in essence, I agreed with. Out of my mother and him, he would be both the more accepting and the more shocked not by what I was doing now, but by what I was thinking. Tucking me up in bed – my God, had anything happened to me worthy of note since then? Tucking me up in bed, I can remember him saying to me, eyes moist with emotion, 'We're the luckiest family in the world.' It seems like he said this many times but it may have only been once or twice. When I asked him why this was, he replied, 'Because we live in England, the best country in the world. It's an island so we don't have poisonous snakes and it never gets too hot or too cold. We live in Surrey, which is the best county in England because it's near enough to London for work and to go to the theatre but far enough away to have green fields and clean air. We have the best size family, because an only child can get lonely and three children always makes one feel left out. And you're a year older than Rachel, so when you're older you can find her boyfriends and she can find you girlfriends.' Then he said in a choked voice, his big face smiling down at me, bristles and pores and curling sideburns in magnified close-up, 'But most of all, we're the luckiest family in the world because we all love each other so much.'

No one could accuse my father of lacking conviction. I can see now that his family seemed perfect to him because he felt so perfectly happy, so blessed, to have it. But growing up, I took this brilliant white version of our family to mean that we should all speak nothing but loving things about each other. Unfortunately, that could make you feel gagged if you harboured resentments or fears, which of course I did.

My parents were of a generation and culture that believed no good could come from putting ideas in people's minds, especially children's. To discuss with me the nuances of my adoptive status could only invite distress. Treat him no different from a natural child and that's how he'll see himself, the entirely honourable and understandable reasoning went. However, distress had already been invited in when I was separated from my birth mother and told I was adopted. (I now use the term "birth mother", having rejected "biological mother" as part of an angrier past.) Closing the lid only trapped those thoughts and feelings inside me.

At the time of first meeting Alison, I was still inclined to blame my parents for how I felt, to see a hidden agenda in their insistence that everything was fine and anyone that thought otherwise was a troublemaker. I thought that what they really felt was I should be grateful for being adopted into their perfect family – into the family of Dad, Mummy and Rachel. Since then, I've attended informal group meetings run by a charity that helps anyone involved in adoption (NORCAP), and the best way to tell instantly the adoptees from the birth mothers and adoptive parents is to include the word "grateful" in what you're saying. Nothing else has quite the same ability to make an adoptee sit up. Grateful for being separated from my birth mother? we think with various degrees of consciousness. Grateful for enabling my adoptive parents to have the family they always wanted? They should be grateful to me!

The truth is that my parents did want me to feel grateful but no more than they wanted Rachel to feel grateful. They wanted us to recognise how lucky we were compared to most people on this planet. Similarly they didn't discuss with me the nuances of being adopted but neither did they discuss with Rachel the nuances of growing up "biological". They didn't believe in making trouble, as they saw it – probably because their parents hadn't invited them to discuss the full breadth of their emotions.

This is a classic example of the doubling rule in operation. They wanted me to be grateful in a normal way and I took it to mean I should be grateful for being adopted. At the time of meeting Alison, I still held a deep resentment about this. I thought my parents had made me feel guilty. They would have denied the very suggestion, I knew, which made me even more resentful. And as if that wasn't enough, I could tell that most people, even my close friends, believed in my parents' innocence.

* * *

The conversation flowed easily enough throughout the drive back to Lorna's farmhouse. Then reality hit. Standing in the drive I told Alison – who looked both faintly ridiculous and endearing, standing there in my figure-hugging turquoise cagoule with her black dress sticking out the bottom – that I'd ring her within the next two days to say if I wanted to meet again.

She asked me to walk with her to the end of the drive and back. I don't know what we talked about, if indeed we did talk. I only remember noticing we weren't holding hands or touching in any way. I asked myself if I was playing games with her, if really I knew the answer I'd give her in two days. If that were the case I should come clean now and put her out of her misery. But I honestly didn't know how I felt. Put another way, I didn't know which of many contradictory feelings I should give priority to.

I realised that, if she were to force me to decide now once and for all, I'd say I didn't want to meet again. Any disappointment I might feel if in due course I realised I'd like to have got to know her more, could never be as grave as the misery I'd inflict on her if I cut and ran after a few meetings once I'd got what I wanted.

I reminded myself what she'd said, almost to herself, as we pulled into the drive a few minutes ago. 'I can't allow hope out, if it's not to be.' She'd said she'd survived up to now by never allowing herself to hope she'd see me again. Hope, as I understood it, was a box she'd placed her feelings for me in, and dropped into the well of her being on the day she handed me over to the adoption association. (Though very likely the box hadn't hit the bottom until Davy and she had realised they couldn't have children of their own.) She'd hauled that box back up on my reappearance, but hadn't yet opened the lid.

Maybe, I thought, she senses the answer I'd give, if pushed, and that's why she hasn't worked harder at getting me to sign on the dotted line.

Arriving at my car, we hugged and I forced myself to slow down, as I opened the door, turned the ignition, looked sideways and waved, and accelerated out of the drive. I drove slowly, without music, enjoying the feel of the wheel, the tilt of the car, as I negotiated country bends. Once, an animal with flashing eyes darted across the road, but otherwise I was alone.

'Don't try and guess what she's feeling,' I said aloud, not even aware I'd been following a train of thought. She seems emotional, which may indicate you get what you see, or it may not. She could be the one to cut her losses after two months knowing you, finding the strain too much, or disillusioned with the preoccupied boy-man she's found compared with the independent, confident adult she expected.

Cut her losses . . . could mean ringing me up in a state to say she can't cope with seeing me any more, the pain, blah blah blah. Or it could mean, and I can remember driving and picturing this in my mind at the same time, though whether I deep down thought it could happen I doubt – a phone call to my parents. The camera tracks my Dad's BMW as they drive through the day to Cornwall, stopping only for petrol. Mummy raps on my front door. My flatmate Greg goes to see who it is, fag in mouth. 'Where's that son of ours?' Mummy growls. 'And you can take that disgusting habit out of your mouth at the same time!'

All I could go on was what I felt this evening. Feelings, feelings, feelings. I sometimes wondered if I even knew what a feeling was, other than something to talk about. I wanted to wedge my fingers into the top of my skull, prise it apart and pull out some brain. Give my mind some room to breathe.

At some point in the journey I pushed play on the cassette panel, piano notes tumbling over each other like speeded-up film of clouds moving across a landscape. Quiet, I told myself. You've done enough for one day. You've done fine. That moment you first entered the lounge and she seemed so far away. You and she stared into each other's eyes, and she said, 'I can't believe it's you.'

'I know,' you said, 'neither can I.' That was a sweet reply, without being puppyish. I think she realised she liked you from then on.

Thomas padding in, asking me, 'Like where are you from James?'

'Her,' you reply. She loved that too. That showed her she could have fun with you. And the way you told that story about the hippie and the café. She saw the journalist/ storyteller in you then. She definitely appreciated the little details that bring a story alive.

I flicked over to the radio, suddenly wanting voices, anyone's other than my own. 'Hello line two,' the DJ said, 'is that Mark from St Austell?' I rested my chest on the steering-wheel. I'd be home in ten minutes. I wanted the day to be over without having to endure one more thought.

3

Shame

An osteopath, ironically recommended by my mother, once observed – during the ringing lull that follows the neck being wrenched sideways – that I'd 'been given away twice'. Once by my birth mother, and a second time by my parents when they sent me to boarding school aged eight. The osteopath considered my bad back to be, at least in part, a symptom of childhood trauma.

This observation of his came at a time before I'd met Alison, when I was writing my second novel, and it naturally pleased me no end. Here was a doctor of sorts, someone who knew my mother, no less, taking my side, confirming my parents as the villains. And he was right, going to boarding school had felt familiar: the disorientation, the loneliness, above all the coping. But there was something about the wording of "given away" that rang false to me. I couldn't buy that I remembered the moment at ten days old of being separated from Alison. It seemed wishful thinking, from my osteopath's point of view, to imagine some cataclysmic event hidden deep in my unconscious. "Wishful" because it suggested the possibility of release, of healing, through alternative medicines such as osteopathy or psychotherapy.

Only recently have I seen around this blind spot. When Alison had told me at the Shipwright's that she'd breastfed me for all ten days that she'd had me 'because I couldn't help it', I'd pushed the anecdote to one side as if she'd told me she'd had a craving for coal or avocados while carrying me. At the time I had focused instead on what she said next, which was that she'd been advised not to breastfeed me by the nurse because it would make giving me away harder for her.

Typical of them, I'd thought, to focus on the adult's loss rather than the child's. Now, however, I think her having breastfed me is an important detail. It means that as a baby I'd have had to make a difficult adjustment from breast milk to formula. But the key point is that it shows how close we were for the first ten days of my life. It seems impossible that I wouldn't have "bonded" with her, to use the psychological jargon.

I believe going to boarding school was traumatic primarily because of the abandonment. Just as I must have yearned for my birth mother's smell, skin and milk after leaving the hospital, so I yearned for my adoptive parents' love and attention when I was sent to boarding school. In this way the abandonment wasn't just about being given away, the rejection, it was also about being away, the missing them.

My parents decided boarding school would be right for me from age eight because I was, in my mother's words, 'so restless' at home and they believed that there I would never run out of things to do or friends to play with. It was also what one did: almost all their friends' children went to public school (private secondary education, usually boarding), and prior to that the majority of the boys also attended prep school (the primary age equivalent of public school). My parents chose Barton House prep school because it came recommended by friends, and because it was near their holiday house in Winbourne, but far enough away from home in Surrey that I wouldn't be tempted to run away or keep wanting to come home for this or that spurious reason.

At elementary school, term-time and holidays seem to go on forever, making the unexpected switch from one to the other like starting a new life. It was during one such endless summer – after my best friend Richard and I had nailed our ties to the Wendy house door to mark our triumphal graduation from elementary school, and before the day in early September when I started at Barton – that I sensed for a moment something was up. A friend of my parents, whose last name I knew to be Carmichael, had come up to my room once I'd gone to bed and told me that Trevor Burman was a good friend of good friends of his.

'Who's Trevor Burman?' I asked.

'Trevor's a good friend of the Rogers,' whoever they were. 'He's the headmaster of your new school.'

Headmaster – what a chilly word that was. My previous headmaster had been called Mr Heath and had pitch black hair and a red face and once I had to stand outside his study, waiting to get the slipper. But for some reason I just got a telling off.

'The Rogers said what a nice man he was,' Carmichael continued.

What did it matter how nice he was? I could only remember speaking to Heath once, during the telling off.

'It's a lovely school . . .'

I suddenly felt very sleepy.

'Plenty of sport . . . Make lots of friends.'

Eventually Carmichael said goodnight and I replied 'Nunnight' in a sweet voice to keep him happy.

This was the first conversation that I can remember having about Barton House, though of course my parents would have told me about it before sending Alan Carmichael to reassure me. Barton House could be said to have entered my consciousness during that conversation. I saw it as a place dominated by one man, Trevor Burman. I think I saw him as like Alan Carmichael: powerful, caring in an impersonal way, and outside the family. But as only very young people can do, where a day is like a week, a week like a year and summer holidays stretch out to infinity, I don't remember giving Trevor Burman and his Barton House any more thought until a trip I took with my mother later that summer to a shop in London.

It was one of those places that hadn't changed in fifty years: dust outlines, piles of boxes and a seedy old man with a moustache and worn areas around the knees and crotch (or have I added that last detail at a later date?) of his worsted trousers. It was a school outfitters; I don't know if it was a normal clothes shop as well, but I think not. My mother led the man around the shop, ticking off items from a list as we bought them. Three grey shirts that looked like they would be itchy, three pairs of long grey wool socks, three pairs of dark grey shorts – three seemed to be the magic number. Two grey V-neck sweaters and one red round-neck jumper that the list said was for 'weekend use'. 'The young man will probably climb trees in it,' was close enough to what the man must have said because I remember thinking that I would be spending my weekends climbing trees, not a pastime I had hitherto indulged in. One blazer, of course, but then two pairs of 'garters' – grey elastic circles to keep your socks from falling down, which you adjusted to the size of your leg by pulling a little buckle one way or the other. There was something foreboding in those garters: nobody at elementary school minded if your socks fell down.

Then the first of three items about which I had to make a choice. Did I want a tuck box with rounded metal corner caps and side clasps or squared off ones? *What was a tuck box for?* I must have asked, because I remember the man telling me it was where you kept your chocolate and all the other things you didn't want other young men 'to get their hands on'. I chose the one with the rounded clasps and the biggest padlock he had. The keys were huge and came on a ring, so that holding them I felt like the jailer in *The Count of Monte Cristo*. The man said the young men gave any spare keys to a teacher and put the ring through their belt so they knew where their key was at all times.

Over to a stack of shelves dedicated to different styles and designs of rug. I looked up and down the shelves and there was no way I could even begin to decide, so Mummy chose a check design in green and black. Finally I would need an "overnight bag". This, the man explained, was because it would take "matron" a little while to unpack 150 young men's trunks and so everyone took enough clothes for the first day in a small bag. Mummy chose a dark grey, really ugly plastic thing that looked like a sports bag, and the man said it would have to be taken away to have my name put on it. That was an empty moment in the mould of the weekend jumper and I seem to remember the man, who was very likely well-meaning and experienced at deflecting panic as well as being seedy, trying to take my mind off the bag's function by saying something like: 'I bet the young man would like a nice big ice cream after all this shopping!'

Even after the trip to the outfitters I still hadn't taken in what boarding school really meant. That last lunch of "spag bol" in the garden at Winbourne, with Auntie Belinda deputising for Dad because he had to be at work – then I was scared, of course, but I still didn't really know what about. I had no details to go on, only new words: prep school and boarding school – why did they have different words for the same thing? – and Trevor Burman. I can't remember much about that short drive to Barton House other than I was in the front seat and Auntie Belinda was in the back, which was like being given a cigar before execution; and the itchy grey trousers that Mummy had insisted I wear in the place of familiar school shorts. If she'd got it wrong and everyone was arriving in shorts – the only attire I could imagine schoolboys in – the humiliation would be horrendous.

Perhaps it was during this journey that my mother introduced the strangest word yet: exeat. I would be going home for the weekend in four weeks and this was called an exeat. A few weeks after that I would be coming home for half-term, which was a whole week long. In descending order of worrying words, it went: exeat, which sounded like day release from prison, overnight bag and then weekend jumper.

You enter the grounds of Barton House from a country lane, turning past iron gates and a small white house with blue trim around the door: a gatehouse. You motor very slowly along a narrow, snaking drive abutted by playing fields, towards a huge building with a porch with pillars and walls extending either side. We parked in front of the porch, where we were greeted by a man, and then walked through huge oak doors into a high-ceilinged hall dominated by a red carpet that swept up a bending staircase. (It was the only time I think I ever went through the main entrance until returning for an old boys' dinner.) Trevor Burman's policy, I later discovered, was to have new boys arrive a few hours before everyone else and greet the parents individually, warmly, and briskly, before sending them back to their cars without their son. This way goodbyes took place in the grand hall and emotions were kept in check, which was preferable for all concerned. It was in any case both too late and too early to be upset.

The next thing I remember is being shown to my dormitory. It had a row of three and a row of four iron beds with mattresses that sank in the middle. Immediately I knew which mine was because on top of one of the beds, in the middle of the row of three, I saw the check rug that my mother had chosen for me at the outfitters. Magically, it seemed, it had found its way onto this bed and had even been made "into" it – the top of the white sheet was folded over and the sides of the rug were tucked in. On the headboard was a sticker saying Mulholland (Oak). (The school was split into four houses, or patrols as they were called at Barton: Oak, Beech, Lime and Elm.) It was a creepy feeling, realising how much of what happened to me went on behind my back. When we were in the outfitters, Mummy, the seedy man, "matron", Trevor Burman – who turned out to have fair hair and fair eyebrows and wore a powder blue jacket, hazy as sand and sea – everyone except me had known where that rug would turn up. I don't think I even thought this unfair, I simply identified it as the way things were. I recognised it with a hollow dread. I acknowledged the familiarity of it. Even as my parents' final words of encouragement lingered in my head, 'You'll soon get used to it, James,' I knew I was being got rid of.

At this point in the story of my school days I can hear my university friend Simon object, 'But surely all children sent to boarding school feel abandoned at the begining, faced with a strange bed? What does it specifically have to do with being adopted?' Like me, Simon went to boarding school aged eight; unlike me, he loved it almost from word go, or claims to have done. I can picture us discussing the matter at the kitchen table in our university flat, as we recharge from a taxing hour watching Robert Kilroy-Silk's daytime talk show.

I address Simon's concern, 'I do not doubt all children sent to boarding school feel some disorientation and rejection. I certainly never thought, *I'm being sent away to boarding school because I'm adopted.* And without remembering *actually thinking* that exact sentence, there's no way I can prove *beyond doubt* that I linked the two things at the time. I believe that I did, though – *subconsciously.*'

Simon looks vexed at my wilful naivety. "'Subconsciously'" – what does that *mean?* Imagining what you think now is what you thought, or "felt", then?'

I ignore him, telling myself he's playing devil's advocate. 'My parents told me they'd "specially chosen" me, right? It was how the adoption association had advised them to word it. And here was a row of beds with names on them...' I pause, letting the imagery take hold. 'I can't say for sure when it was I began picturing my parents "specially choosing" me from a row of beds, but I reckon there's a good chance the idea was triggered by entering that dormitory for the first time.

'It's even possible,' I go on, warming to my theme, 'it's even possible I'd been imagining a row of beds from when my parents first used the words "specially chosen" – before I ever knew about Barton. In that case the dormitory fitted an existing picture, making it even more frightening.'

I realise I don't feel remotely frightened as I say this. As so often happens, especially after watching daytime chat shows like *Kilroy*, our conversation has moved swiftly from the personal to the theoretical. 'Whenever it was I first got the idea of a row of beds, I don't think there's any doubt I connected arriving at Barton with being given away.' I stop, aware I've failed to convince Simon of the non-existence of doubt. (I haven't come up with the doubling rule yet – coined in conjunction with a therapist I'll later see – to explain the way the adoptee looks for signs of rejection. And without the term, I find the psychological process impossible to put into words satisfactorily.)

'It's interesting how you take the negative interpretation of "specially chosen",' Simon says. 'You could have taken it to mean what your parents had meant by it, which was that being adopted made you special. Unlike with most children, where parents get what they're given.' His voice softens, clearly touched by the idea.

'So you're saying I deliberately misunderstood my parents, at age three, or whenever I was first told I was adopted?'

Simon has known me long enough not be put off course by a rise in temperature. 'What I'm saying is that you are deliberately misunderstanding your parents now, so you can blame them for your failings as an adult. Who knows what you thought aged three!'

He has a point, but I pretend to be hurt. Make it seem as if he'll never know the torment an adoptee goes through. I smile bravely, showing him how lucky he is to have such a quality person as a friend.

'Your parents sent you to prep school,' Simon continues, 'precisely because they wanted to treat you like a normal child. They actually saw you as no different from their friends' sons. Think how much worse it would've been if they'd compensated for your being adopted by keeping you at home.'

I concede that my parents were damned if they treated me normally, damned if they treated me differently. 'But it's hard not to feel,' I go on, 'that any parent that sends their children to boarding school, especially prep school, is opting out of a portion of child-rearing. What do they do while parents with children at day school are picking them up at different times and from different places, then helping them with, or at least supervising, all the different homeworks – at the same time as cooking supper and perhaps making something different for hubby when he comes in?' I shake Frosties into a bowl and, adding milk, supply the answer: 'They drink G'n'Ts with friends that also have children in boarding school.'

Simon laughs. 'That's the whole point of having money. Rich parents with children at day school get the gardener to collect the kids from football or ballet, and the daily help to prepare a meal and check that little Johnny and Deborah are getting on with their homework.'

Satisfied there's nothing more to be said on the subject, Simon tries another tack: 'You've got this rosy picture of day school, as if it would be like in *The Waltons*. I suspect the families on *Kilroy* are nearer the truth. I liked the fact that coming home was special, that my parents were actually looking forward to seeing me after a month away. And I was looking forward to seeing them. Instead of being at each other's throats over homework and wanting lifts. Why do you refuse to acknowledge the positive side?'

'I can see the positive side now,' I say, 'theoretically. But I'm talking about how I felt at the time.'

'But what you think now,' Simon says, 'is important because' – his eyes travel to the clock, which reminds us that *Neighbours* is about to start – 'it tells you that ev-er-y-one waaaaaaaaaas –' his voice, rising to its highest note, hangs there, a biplane at the top of its climb, before descending steeply but confidently, 'doing – their – best.'

Ber-boom. Absolute certainty, aged twenty. That he's right, I have no doubt. But I also think I might have a point too. We're tacitly agreed on one thing, though, that the discussion can wait until we've been brought up to date with the latest, much cooler dilemmas facing lovely Kylie and poor Jason.

*   *   *

My first night at Barton was dominated by one thing: I must not wet my bed. Nothing was more important. The starched white sheets I was lying between were the ceiling and floor of my world. I'd swallowed a Tofronil, the pellet-like pill that was meant to stop me sleeping too heavily, enabling me to wake up before I peed. But I couldn't remember the last time I'd woken up at home in the middle of the night and walked to the bathroom in dry pyjamas. Sometimes I woke up as I was peeing, which was even worse. I'd strip the bed and use the sheet to sponge up any wetness on the plastic under-sheet, then carry it to the bathroom in a ball, drop it in the bath and take a replacement from the linen cupboard. If I was sleeping over at Richard's, a plastic under-sheet would be packed in my bag for his mum to put secretly in place on the camp bed before Richard and I went up to his room for the night. It was a work of art getting into that bed, with Richard a few feet away, without making a crumpling noise.

But this was different. At least there was no plastic sheet. Nobody spoke that first night at Barton, once the lights had been turned out by a woman in a cardigan. It was still light outside but with the curtains drawn it was dark enough to be able to pretend you were asleep.

Later, an older boy came in. Through half-closed eyes I watched him take off his clothes and place them folded on the wood chair beside his bed, like we'd all done, then put on his pyjamas and slither between his sheets. He hadn't said a word to anyone. In fact, the next sound I heard was a loud bell. It was morning, and my pyjamas and sheets were damp and cold when I moved.

I carefully got out of bed, keeping the sheets and rug pulled up. Luckily the yellow stain remained hidden. I can't remember anything else specifically about my first day at Barton. No doubt we were shown our form room, met our teacher Miss Harris, and wrote our names on the front of exercise books. Some games would have been played. But I can still feel the damp pyjamas that I stepped into that night, and the cold, musty sheets I slid between.

I felt absolutely no self-pity, only despair checked by quiet rage at my body's failure. Each night added another yellow stain, so that like the rings of a tree trunk you could tell how many nights it was before the sheets were changed. Clean sheets, what luxury! And so it went on, week after week dominated by pee and fear, frustration and self-disgust. My mother told me many years later that she'd discussed my bedwetting with Jill Burman, the headmaster's wife, prior to my arrival and Mrs Burman had thought it best to ignore it. That way I wouldn't think anyone knew and my pride would be intact. Well, at least that showed they'd thought about it.

When I picture myself lying in my own urine, alone and afraid, I don't see how I can't have recalled on a basic emotional level lying eight years earlier in a strange cot without my birth mother, inexplicably severed from the person who had been my sole reason for living. And as I picture myself in that dual state – a baby in an eight-year-old body – I realise there's nothing more to be said about it. It happened and it felt very bad and I don't care about why it was allowed to happen or how many worse things are done to other children.

It was only while researching the sociological context for this book that I began to be able to place my intense early experiences in a wider setting. Following research in America during the 1980s, clinical psychologist David Kirschener found that adoptees often exhibited similar personality traits. To define the most extreme of these – rebellion, truancy, sexual promiscuity and trouble with the law – he coined the term "adopted child syndrome". Although this condition clearly didn't fit me, I felt I was onto something. Here was confirmation from the medical world that I was part of a continuum – albeit at the law-abiding end – linking all adoptees through a shared experience. Perhaps Alexander the Great and Charles Dickens, both adoptees, had also wet their beds in subconscious protest. Our most outrageous brothers and sisters even had a syndrome named after them!

Working at the same time as Kirschener, American psychologist David Brodzinsky produced research that informs much of today's thinking on the sociological effects of adoption. In his 1993 report, *Long-term Outcomes in Adoption*, he states that a series of studies carried out by him and his colleagues on children in non-clinical settings (that is, children in the general community) found that 'six to twelve-year-old adopted children manifested more adjustment problems than their non-adopted peers'. Teachers rated the adopted children as scoring lower than non-adopted children in all areas, which included independent learning, school involvement and academic achievement. When parents were asked, adopted boys came out as more likely than non-adopted boys to be rated within a maladaptive range of uncommunicative behaviour (20 per cent versus 4.6 per cent) and hyperactivity (8.2 per cent versus 0 per cent); and adopted girls were found to exceed non-adopted girls in symptomatology related to depression (13.9 per cent versus 3 per cent), hyperactivity (13.9 per cent versus 0 per cent) and aggression (10.8 per cent versus 0 per cent).

Brodzinsky's study follows a cross-sectional design, in that it compares the behaviour of adopted and non-adopted children of the same age range and at the same time. But this kind of study gives no indication of how well each person "adjusts" as they grow up. For this information, we must turn to longitudinal studies, which measure groups of people at different ages.

All three longitudinal studies cited in Brodzinsky's report show the same broad trend: adopted pre-teen children have a higher measurement of confidence and achievement than pre-teens in long-term foster care and a lower measurement than non-adopted pre-teens living with their birth parents. By the time these same people become teenagers, the gap between adopted and non-adopted is closing fast, and is widening between these two groups and those teenagers in long-term foster care. And once they are adults, those brought up in long-term foster care fare by far the worst, while no discernible gap exists between adoptees and non-adoptees.

The findings of longitudinal studies are often cited by those wishing to downplay the psychological risk associated with adoption. The implication is that adoptees generally have a wobble in childhood but few suffer long-term damage.

However, as Brodzinsky points out, longitudinal studies

have inherent methodological problems. By the time interviewees reach adulthood they have been measured three or four times and may have become "test-wise", knowing the "right" answer to give. Longitudinal studies also have the effect of "selective dropout": those who continue to participate with the research to the adult stage are likely to be more motivated and generally better adjusted than a random sample of individuals.

Brodzinsky concludes, 'Taken as a whole, the research literature generally supports the view that adoptees are at an increased risk for behavioural, psychological and academic problems compared with non-adopted individuals. However, the majority of adoptees are well within the normal range of adjustment.' In other words, we can't keep using being adopted as a never-ending excuse.

When other variables are considered, results are often inconclusive. Some studies say male adoptees do worse than female, others find no difference. Some say adoptees in mixed families (with both adopted and "biological" children) do better than those in all-adoptee families, others find the opposite to be the case. No firm conclusions can be drawn about the effect on an adoptee of being a first, middle, youngest or only child in his adoptive family.

A firm conclusion does seem possible on one variable: the older the adoptee at the time of placement, the higher the risk of psychological problems. However, by itself this finding is both too general and too predictable to be of much interest. Studies so far have failed to introduce effectively another, crucial variable: the quality of the adoptee's life before being placed for adoption. It stands to reason that an adoptee placed at the age of four who has been passed from foster home to foster home, or who has been abused, will have a higher risk of psychological problems than one who has stayed with the same foster carer. The problem with trying to factor in this variable, or bundle of variables, must be that it is so hard to quantify.

The same presumably applies to the quality of the adoptee's life after he has been adopted. What does it matter if the adoptee is the oldest son in a mixed family or the youngest daughter in an all-adoptee family, compared to whether the adoptive parents loved the child – or even compared to whether the child was bullied at school?

Of course, you can make statistics say more or less anything if you try hard enough. But both designs of study, whether cross-sectional or longitudinal, agree on this: at primary school age – the time I was at Barton – adoptees appear to be more psychologically vulnerable than their non-adopted peers. Brodzinsky extrapolates, 'At this age, most children begin to understand the meaning and implications of being adopted. As children's knowledge of adoption deepens, so do their feelings of anxiety and confusion about their family status.'

* * *

Before breakfast at Barton, everyone would assemble on the tarmac in front of the porch. There were four lines, one for each patrol. A middle-aged, burly man was in charge. Mr Franks, or Fred as he was known behind his back, was a retired petty officer in the Navy and his principal role at the school was discipline. He could appear somewhere even before trouble had begun. He was actually quite a shy man, as I found out at the old boys' dinner, but to those still at the school he was not to be crossed. Fred's standard rebuke was a cuff around the back of the head, which for those watching looked like a Bjorn Borg topspin forehand with the boy's head as the ball.

When Fred was good and ready he would order the head of each patrol to lead his charges in a circular walk around the grounds, taking in the concrete pond for sailing toy boats in, the Burmans' new red brick house – which included a small dormitory where older boys stayed for a term at a time – a games pitch and an uninterrupted view of the Barton House façade. On Sundays, the morning walk was exchanged for *teethinirs*, where you lined up in patrols in the Red Passage and had your knees, nails, teeth and ears inspected for cleanliness by Mrs Burman or Matron. The damage done to tender eardrums as, carrying out a final check in the bathroom, we wrapped a handkerchief around the handle of our toothbrush, spat on the end and stirred it around inside our ear holes, should start to emerge at Preparatory Schools' Boys for the Hard of Hearing reunions in the next decade or so.

There were new words to add to those unsettling ones I'd discovered before arriving. *Teethinirs*, I only found out in my last year, was really *teeth'n'ears*. If you didn't like someone for any reason at all, they were 'spastic'. Then we were told in assembly by Burman that spastic children couldn't help it and anyone heard using the word disrespectfully would get one hour's detention, the maximum you could get, and spastic quickly became the high-stakes, big occasion insult. If you didn't want to do something or didn't like the way something had been handled by a teacher it was 'wet', which sounds innocuous enough but try saying it under your breath in Mrs Burman's hearing after she's told you off for something. Mrs Burman could make Fred look like Mother Teresa. And there was the word 'complex', drawn out in a sneering voice into three syllables, as 'Com-ple-ex', and addressed to anyone that couldn't take a joke no matter how insulting, unfair and unfunny.

My best friend Harvey was a skinny boy whose love of tree-climbing would have delighted the shop assistant at the school outfitters – though I don't remember ever seeing Harvey hanging from a branch in his "red weekend jumper". I once followed him up a tree and threw myself like a monkey from branch to branch in every way like Harvey, except when it came to holding onto one of the lower branches.

Apparently I landed on the ground on my head. Harvey later told me he'd swung his way down the tree and run to fetch help while a group of boys stood around me in a circle, believing I was dead. The very moment that Fred arrived, I jumped to my feet, grinning stupidly. Fred of course thought the whole thing was a set up and anyway osteopathy, chiropractice, shiatsu, yoga, acupuncture, sports physiotherapy or even cognitive psychotherapy, all of which I've sampled since then in varying degrees, were not exactly the modus operandi of a small Sussex prep school in the 1970s. Better to assume I was following the naughty-boy-rises-to-captain-of-industry model of development. In fact, I was unlucky not to get a Fred cuff round the back of the head, which would certainly have sent me to the hospital I undoubtedly should have gone to in the first place.

Harvey and I shared a need for secrecy, a place of our own. We each had a biscuit tin which we filled with important possessions and then ceremoniously buried in neighbouring holes in the Junior Woods (each Year had their own patch of trees in the grounds). Items I remember carefully arranging in my tin included chocolate, a lighter, a notepad with passwords and codes in it, a Parker pen I'd stolen from another boy and a penknife I'd persuaded a malleable elderly friend of my parents to let me buy at Chessington Zoo. Sometimes we would go to our tins together, sometimes I would go by myself. The best time was after dark when we had to rely on night vision to find our tins and open them. Using my lighter to see by, we tucked into a square of chocolate each, like commandos in a foxhole deep inside enemy territory.

One Sunday evening, Fred couldn't find one of us and sent search parties of prefects into the grounds to hunt us down. Under cover of trees and bushes, we advanced along the northern perimeter silent as ghosts, ran in a crouch across a playing field to the rear of the cricket pavilion, and then sprinted for the changing rooms in the blind spot between approaching and retreating search parties. Fred eventually caught up with us playing table tennis in the basement and we apologised for completely losing track of time.

The basement was a whole floor of windowless rooms with exposed pipes and flickering strip lights. In this dusty netherworld were located showers, changing rooms, a large area with wall-to-wall shelves where each boy's tuck box was stored, some table tennis rooms, and a laundry room, which was out of bounds, containing industry-sized washing machines and a tumble-drier. It was down in this basement that I indulged in my most secret, and solitary, activity.

It all started when I saw a boy's woollen vest hanging on a peg in a changing room. I waited for everyone to leave and then touched it, felt it. It was soft and still warm from contact with his skin. The musky smell gave me a cosy feeling. The label said *St Michael*. Above it was the boy's nametag: *W. Allan*. He was a year above me, a bit of a wimp, by which I meant he didn't play sports all day long like me. I liked the off-white colour, the round neck and the narrow sleeves with a frilly edge that protruded from each shoulder like little wings. Encased in it you would always be snug and warm (not that I was ever physically cold in my own clothes). At that moment I began an obsession, you could say love affair, with other boys' woollen underwear. Instinctively I knew that it wouldn't be the same to get my mother to buy me my own – it had to be someone else's.

Clothes were kept on labelled shelves in a storeroom on the first floor, so I could pretend to be going up to my dormitory to fetch something, then dart in, take what I wanted and put it on at my leisure in a nearby toilet. I discovered that St Michael did woollen pants to go with the vest. You could tuck the vest into the pants, which had a naturally high waist, and feel completed protected. I was eight years old, pre-pubescent, but the feel of the soft brushed wool stroking my thighs as I pulled up the pants was the height of sensuality. In that woollen case I felt lovable. On an emotional level I understood that boys with St Michael woollen underwear must have mothers that wanted them to feel snug and safe. It was evidence that what was inside such boys was worth protecting, was deserving of special love. I suppose that in their underwear I could imagine I was one of those boys.

Once, I was shinning up the metal pole that supported a concrete porch outside the toilets. Don't ask me why I was doing this; probably, to use Mallory's reason for climbing Everest, because it was there. Suddenly a wonderful tingly feeling spread through my body. I had no idea how it happened or even where it came from. But there was something so intensely private about the experience that I didn't tell anyone about it. Apart from anything else, I didn't want other boys using my magic pole. But whenever the coast seemed clear I would have a quick climb, treating it, I suppose, like a Frenchman stopping at a bar for *un express*.

Imagine the pleasure when it dawned on me I could climb the pole in woollen underwear. It was like dropping a shot of cognac into the *express*. A nice little lift – unless you're up the top of the pole, mid-tingle, and Fred passes by.

'What're you doing up there, son?'

'N – n – oth – i – i – ing, s – s – sir.'

'You'd better come down before you hurt yourself.' I suspect Fred knew what was going on and decided to spare my blushes, because he walked away without waiting to give my head a cross-court topspin forehand.

Needless to say that was the last time I climbed the pole. But I still had underwear. At some point I began hanging it on a pipe behind the boiler, deep in the dusty bowels of the basement. Soon there was quite a collection and I began to discriminate between items according to their original owner. Small sweet obviously petted boys' woollen underwear gave greater satisfaction than that belonging to larger, brasher boys like myself. Puberty had arrived and I was deriving a distinctly sexual thrill from my obsession. I would put the underwear on, grab hold of a high pipe running along the boiler room wall and pull myself up and down so that I rubbed against the rough brick. Gradually I developed a worn patch on the flies of my shorts. In my first year at public school I dropped the woollen aspect altogether and favoured the underwear, whatever the fabric and design, of boys that were classically pretty – or lush, as they were unashamedly called – although they still had to seem sensitive or at least have a shy side. In this way I maintained a rotating collection of around two or three items.

Gay? I suppose it was, in the sense that most young men go through a period of fascination with other boys' bodies at the beginning of puberty, usually referred to as "a gay phase" (the current politically correct term is same-gender attracted youth). Public school girls, I know through listening to my sister and her friends, go through a female version of this phase, referring to an older girl that they admire as a "pash", short for passion.

I believe, however, there is a second explanation for my obsession with wearing other boy's underwear that is distinct from, and at the same time related to, a developmental stage in puberty. I think it was an attempt by me to be someone else, perhaps the biological son of my parents that they had tried so hard to treat me as. Or perhaps I wanted to be the boy that, as a baby, would have so captivated his birth mother that she would have been unable to give him away. If your outer clothes tell others how you want to be seen, perhaps these inner clothes told me how I wanted to feel. In them I could travel far away from urine-soaked sheets, to a land of snuggly duvets, unguarded affection and magical hard-ons.

Soon after arriving at public school, a new, equally absorbing interest in pornography, involving pictures of women, was initiated when I found a magazine on top of a toilet cistern. Tucked under my jumper, the magazine left the cubicle and made its way to my dormitory unobserved, where it was deftly palmed under my mattress.

It was this hiding place that gave me the idea to look under other mattresses when I was next alone in the dormitory. I moved a selection of the publications that I found – many of which made my first acquisition look like a Ladybird book – to under my own mattress. A few days later, they were gone. But it didn't take me long to retrieve them and find more besides under a variety of mattresses in dormitories across both landings; and when they too were "borrowed", as I began to view such disappearances, I only had to go on a five minute sortie to assemble a fresh collection.

This new obsession was a great relief to me because it proved I was growing into a normal, heterosexual male. Somehow my desire for gum-chewing "towny" girls, who all seemed sluttish to my blinkered, sex-obsessed mind, and for my sister's friends in Alice bands and tight V-neck sweaters, who all seemed painfully unobtainable, failed to reassure me where these predictable, dehumanised images succeeded. Graduating from other boys' underwear to porn also meant leaving behind the hideous fear of being caught *en flagrant délit sous-vêtements de laine*. At prep school I had nightmares of tripping over, knocking myself out and having to be undressed. 'What have we got here, matron?' I could hear Mrs Burman saying, holding up the offending nametag for all to see.

That particular time bomb only went off once. In my last year at Barton I decided to leave an anonymous note, written in pencil with my left hand, saying I'd now stopped taking underwear. I'm not sure if I hoped this would force me to do so or if I knew the finger of blame would point at me if underwear stopped disappearing the day I left. I chose to leave the note in the laundry room, my primary source of woollen booty since discovering that unlike cotton underwear it couldn't be tumble-dried and had to be hung out to dry.

Burman called me into his study, where his wife was already seated, waiting. This was the same study where I'd consumed quantities of squash and cake after obliterating Ballard Hill at tennis. This was the same man who'd personally congratulated me on my "exceptional" performance in the rugby sevens competition that Barton won for the first time in our history. Once I'd knocked down Sompting Manor's huge black winger he lost his mystique both for us and his own team. 'Every time after that,' Burman had told me as if he were entrusting me with the code for King Solomon's mines, 'when he set off on one of his runs, he always had in the back of his mind: *I hope that forward doesn't tackle me again.*'

When Burman asked me if I was the one who'd written the note left in the laundry room, I felt confident in replying that I wasn't sure what he was talking about. I don't know if Burman had or was planning to ask other boys the same question, if I'd been his prime suspect, or if indeed he'd instinctively known it was me and was giving me the opportunity to come clean, have a cry and then a talk with his (frightening) wife. Whatever his strategy, it bore no fruit. Mrs Burman tried to outwit me by asking me how to spell "intention", a word I'd deliberately misspelt in the note. When I calmly told her the correct spelling I think that she began to believe me, though I am not so sure about canny Burman. For my part, I was growing in confidence. I think I felt as if I hadn't done it. How could a well-liked, sporting hero be interested in sissy woollen underwear? The boy who did that was someone else, not the real me. I felt no guilty pang when I said, 'I may be able to help you if you tell me what's prescribed on the note.' I could see that he didn't want to read it out, perhaps he was embarrassed. He hadn't yet made any mention of underwear, after all. And I was pleased with the word "prescribed", it made me sound like a lawyer, I felt, on his level. (Hearing myself say it now, I realise it's the one moment when I conclusively give myself away: I'm too confident.)

Burman dismissed me with a poker face, refusing to be drawn into any duplicity and, I want to say, muck, but I'm not sure he would have called it that. He'd been in the business too long to be shocked by something like this, most likely.

My victory in Burman's study supported the idea that the real James was the public one, and that the secret James was the clever one. The trick was to ensure the two were kept separate. Unfortunately this became near impossible when my parents entered the picture.

Saturday afternoons at Barton were an occasion for parents to visit their sons on site. Mother and father watched their pride-and-joy get worked over on the rugby pitch or torpedoed in the future generations by a cricket ball (boxes were for 1st XI only), before leading their little hero back to the car, parked somewhere along the curving drive. Food was then dispensed in lieu of parental attention during the week. Meaningful conversation was impossible. You talked about the match or things your parents had got up to during the week. Each crisp took you one crunch nearer to the moment you had to climb out of your car and watch it glide out of view. Standing on the drive the secret self wrapped his cold arms around you. He had always been there, like a clammy fog surrounding the car, while you kept him at bay with chocolate and warm cans of Top Deck.

I was still fairly new at Barton when my parents first came, watched and, I discovered, parked too near the main building. It was like having a picnic in Waterloo Station. Passers-by peered in to match boy with car; you could even see us from a classroom. Of course I didn't say anything, I just ate. Mummy probably talked about Auntie Belinda taking brass rubbing classes or my aunt letting my cousin paint his bedroom battleship grey. Suddenly a round, smirking, needy face appeared between two conifers in front of us. He was lying on his stomach and he looked straight into our car, at us. His name was James Dixon and he was nice enough but I did not want him in my car. This was a holy place. But James, I could see, was choosing not to respect such values. (Soon, our parents would start talking on a touchline, realise they had things in common and become friends. A few years after that I would stay with his family during an entire half-term while mine were away and his parents would make me feel like part of the family. However, I would never be close to James.)

My mother couldn't resist the allure of the fly and, as a weak smile played across James Dixon's face, lunged with a long sigh followed by, 'What's his name, James? We must give him something.' Whether she felt sorry for him, was trying to help me make a friend or even believed we had enough happiness to go around, I don't know. He ended up in the back with Mummy, scoffing orange Clubs and salt and vinegar crisps. Mummy wanted to know where he lived, what his hobbies were – he had a rabbit that died – if he had any brothers and sisters . . . *You kept going, saying nothing, because to stop was to look into an abyss.*

I'm going too far? I don't think so. Compared with being a starving child in Africa, Barton's miseries don't register. But by that rationale no part of British society warrants complaint: sink estates and failing comprehensives are like living in *The Sound of Music* compared to a Rio slum. If we can accept that misery exists on a sliding scale, we must accept that all misery is worth our attention. If not, who is qualified to set the minimum standard?

Barton was far from constant misery. I had a dull awareness of being abandoned, medicated by woollen underwear, occasionally becoming a sharp pain when the worlds of school and home interfaced. I know an adult man who to this day refuses to get in a car on a Sunday evening because it reminds him of the drive back to boarding school.

As you got older you knew what to expect and parting became easier. No doubt the doubling rule continued to operate at the moment of abandonment (experienced as rejection) as well as afterwards (the loneliness). But I suspect few Barton boys would cite watching their parents drive away at the end of an exeat as the highpoint of their childhoods.

Strangely, coming home could be as unsettling as going back. I can remember entering the lounge where Rachel was watching *Crackerjack* and perching uncertainly on the arm of the sofa. I had entered a foreign country, where you watched some TV after homework with some juice and a chocolate biscuit. Mentally I was still at Barton, where Home at mealtimes was represented by your personal jar of jam or honey. Of course I knew that Rachel would eventually be sent away to boarding school too (aged 14, because she was a girl), but I still couldn't help feeling like a servant in the presence of the lady of the house.

4

Guilt

Alison and her husband Davy's pub had won national awards, which meant holiday-makers and "white settlers" – second-home owners from east of the border – came out of their way to visit. A cosy wood-beamed bar led through on one side to a restaurant decorated with seafaring knick-knacks and paintings by a local artist, and on the other side to a long thin family room, once a stable, from where children that ventured out were met by a stern look from Davy behind the bar, ensuring a speedy return to their Plasticine and cardboard books. Davy had a large stomach on a medium frame, wore a red kerchief knotted around his neck and appeared to puff on one of his pipes more or less continuously. He had a deadpan sense of humour that, used on rowdy or unsuitably-dressed customers, invariably had them retreating sheepishly to the picnic tables outside. His kingdom was the bar, as Alison's was the restaurant.

The head chef, Nigel, could multitask. Scribbling notes, chopping, calling orders, watching timers, turning mushrooms, skewering joints, bantering, humming, tasting and basting, all were completed like speeded-up tai chi. This was his first position after graduating in catering at the same college where I was studying journalism, and Alison liked to engage him and the other young men under him, all of whom were surfers, in badinage as they prepared fresh crab salads, grilled fish of the day with glazed carrots, and roasted lamb shank with rosemary and dauphinoise potatoes. 'Wonderful fish today, Nigel – wonderful,' she'd say. Where Davy was ironic, Alison was earnest, gushing (like me, in that way). A sentence without a heavily stressed word wasn't worth saying.

Nigel agrees that the sole is nice today.

'You out surfing this morning, Tim?' Alison asks the commis chef.

'He took a drink, Alison,' Nigel says, his knife a blur of steel, slices of onion collapsing in a perfect fan.

'I wondered why you looked so tired this morning!' Alison chirps, deliberately misunderstanding Nigel, who's referring to Tim taking a mouthful of sea water while out surfing.

I wasn't sure if these conversations were for my benefit and if, when I wasn't there, Alison simply said, 'Make sure we order some more of that lemon sole, Nigel,' and Nigel made a noise in the affirmative. Naturally I derived a secret pleasure from entering the charts at number one while all the other young men had to work their way up steadily in Alison's estimation. No chopping vegetables or ordering fish for me: I wandered into the kitchen with a pint of ale in my hand that I'd poured for myself "on the house" and asked for a crab sandwich or steak and chips as the mood took me. To be fair, I picked up no inkling of resentment from any of the staff, who, if anything, seemed pleased for Alison. And for my part, being special and odd at the same time was home from home – I could perform the role, and feel the attendant self-loathing, standing on my head.

Special and odd meant I didn't need the fried breakfast, didn't need Alison, didn't even need to be a journalist (financially this was true, at least in the short term, thanks to the trust fund set up by my father). I had alighted from my space ship in West Cornwall to beguile the locals with my self-deprecating humour and freedom from the constraints of everyday living. Here more than ever, where the first thing people knew about me – before I even knew of their existence – was that I was Alison's "son" given up for adoption, I could be special and odd almost without lifting a finger. Make way, Very Adopted Person coming through. I was Bottom lolling in the fairy kingdom while all about me fellow humans fretted over the mundanities of existence.

After our first meeting Alison had been so worried I would disappear without trace, she'd rung the college to make sure I was really enrolled there. (I'd told Lorna my surname during a lapse of discretion and she'd passed it on to Alison.) In fact, Alison had been at the point of driving to the college, she subsequently told me, to try and intercept me on the way out of a lecture – when I phoned to say that I'd like to meet again.

It had been talking on the phone with my university friend Fiona that had finally persuaded me. Up until then I'd been on balance in favour of not meeting again. I'd satisfied my curiosity, I told myself, my fears were allayed. I came from a real woman who was sane and capable. Further information could only muddy the waters. What did I want another mother for? When the novelty wore off, which it surely would in a matter of months, I'd be left with two old ladies to look after in twenty years' time, two sponge cakes to eat and two lawns to mow. I also knew it would be cruel to meet once or twice more, begin to develop a bond, and then break it off. It would have to be one meeting or – how many? What could I realistically get away with in the long run: a surreptitious phone call around Christmas and a trip to Cornwall every two or three years? She might decide to move to the South-East to be nearer me! I was getting that trapped feeling already.

With no phone in my rented accommodation, I'd rung Fiona from a booth in the street. Now a professional actor, she had played the lead part in several university productions in which I'd performed utility roles and we had been mates ever since. Where my male friends would want to get to the advice bit as quickly as possible, I knew Fiona would be equally happy savouring the details of my amazing news.

As I told her the story of how I met Alison, I noticed I was already finding ways to strengthen the dramatic impact. It worked better to start in the middle of the story with a description of when Alison and I first laid eyes on each other and then flash back to meeting Mrs Williams, who, in the space of a few days, seemed to have gained a broad Cornish accent and shaky limbs, no doubt in the interests of defining her soothsaying role. And Alison, to avoid scoring cheap points, was no longer too large for my cagoule – or was I unintentionally jumping to the defence of my gene pool? But it was the ending that caused the most difficulty. I couldn't see how to get the narrative arc to glide to a satisfying conclusion, order restored. There was no way to disguise the fact that the story so far ended on a cliff-hanger. I had done something that could not be undone; emotional upheaval was bound to follow.

The story of how I met Alison was now ready for editing. All subsequent tellings would refer back, no matter how subconsciously, to this performance. Thoughts, emotions, dialogue, setting, characterisation, would forever use this version, spoken to Fiona down a telephone line, as their primary source. The live moment had officially been superseded by the story. And Fiona, the first audience, would have co-created the way those events were remembered.

I told her that bumping into Mrs Williams and then Lorna on my first visit to Treven Bay had shown me how small a place Cornwall was. My parents had two sets of close friends with cottages in Cornwall, though hopefully they only mixed with other white settlers. But sooner or later my parents would find out. And the way coincidences were obediently queuing up, chances were my parents wouldn't even need a white settler friend to tip them off about what their son had really been up to on that journalism course.

Fiona, the actor, is unable to resist improving the scene. 'Your mother's having her hair done in Knightsbridge. Her stylist says, "Did you see that programme last night about adoption, Mrs Mulholland?" And the lady in the chair next to your mum hears what they're talking about and says to her stylist "I heard an amazing story about adoption from an old friend of mine who lives in Cornwall, Doreen Williams . . .".'

'It could happen,' I whimper down the phone.

'And then?' Fiona asks, in sparring Method Actor mode.

'I risk emotional excommunication for wilfully seeking a second mother. To make matters worse, I did it behind their backs. And what's more, if Alison and I were spotted together in London,' for some reason I picture us in a wine bar, 'I would have done it in their own back yard.' I can hear my mother warning me as a child, 'It's always better to tell the truth in the first place, James, than let us find out for ourselves.'

It dawns on me suddenly, the real reason why I've chosen to ring Fiona rather than a male friend. Intuitively I must have known she would point me in the direction I already wanted to go in. Even though we appear to be discussing if I should meet Alison again, what I'm really angling for is for her to give me the go-ahead to do so – to share in the responsibility.

One lingering concern, I tell Fiona, is the fundamental difference between Alison and my situation. I already have a mother, whereas I'm Alison's only son. From my point of view, I'm not sure if I would ever be able to see her as my mother, or even an aunt figure. At the moment she seems to be a way of gaining a sensation of independence from my parents, albeit without their knowing. Considering our different agendas, is it even possible for us to have a successful relationship?

Fiona tells me not to worry about meetings number three, ten or 42. What matters is whether I want to meet Alison once more. Is my curiosity completely satiated? Have I asked her everything I want to know? Do I even know if I like her? To see her only once, Fiona seems to be suggesting, would be like drawing the curtain after the first scene. Intriguing, but hardly satisfying.

*   *   *

So we meet again, spending the first of many evenings in the sitting room of Davy and Alison's flat above the pub. Looking back, I seem remarkably, suspiciously at home. Alison commented on it after our first of a series of Sunday lunches (attended in turn by Lorna, brothers, nephews and nieces and their offspring), saying, 'It felt as if you've always been part of the family.' And it did. I was revelling in the attention, in my chance to play the wounded adoptee to a captive audience. I knew somewhere inside me I must feel resentment, I just wasn't able or didn't wish to find it. Alison once even came out and asked me if I felt angry at her for giving me away and I replied that strangely I didn't. I later even told her, attempting to explain away my lack of venom, that I'd "forgiven" her. She looked at me with moist eyes, but I could tell she didn't really believe me.

The journalism course was peopled with twenty-something graduates like myself. There were parties hosted in a rented farmhouse and in damp flats last furnished in the 1970s, and evenings spent getting pissed in pubs, before driving back to our lodgings, five packed into a rusting Escort or Polo, music blaring. I quickly got my shorthand to 90 words per minute but, like others in my class, found those last ten words infuriatingly elusive. National and local government had its moments, but journalism law was fascinating, learning about contempt of court and precedents set in the wake of unscrupulous publications. This was what journalism seemed to be all about, rolling in the gutter or pulling down a US president.

One guy on the course wanted to return to Colombia where he'd been on holiday, to write a day-in-the-life piece on a rock of crack-cocaine, trace its journey from coca leaf to crack pipe. The last someone heard of him, journalism was a letdown and he was delivering pizzas in Lewisham. Most of us went on to local papers, where you could expect a starting salary of £8,900 per annum. I won't say at this point where I ended up, but I will say it wasn't at *The Times*.

In the early evenings or weekends I went for walks along the cliffs. My favourite was one near St Agnes, Porth-something. You crept in neutral down a steep slope to a small cove, where you parked in front of a trailer café that made delicious toasted baguettes filled with warm garlicky mushrooms topped with melted cheese. The coast is littered with old mines and nooks and crannies to explore. You could peer over the edge and watch for ages as waves swooped into a crevice, back-flipped and returned to the ocean. I met a young man, Christopher, also walking the cliffs, who had completed the same journalism course as me the year before. He had stayed in the area after attaining a post at a local paper. What was worrying me at the time was how you found your stories. I asked him if it wasn't a terrible strain not knowing week after week if you'd be able to find enough copy to fill your space in the paper?

Christopher reassured me that once you had enough contacts, it was deciding which stories to leave out. There was always a parish meeting or opening of something if you were desperate.

But I'm an *enfant terrible*, I felt like replying, I don't want to have to spend my weekends at village fêtes. What concerned me about all this journalism business was that it would eat into my free time. Not that I did anything particularly wonderful during my evenings and weekends, it was just that they were mine and I wanted them all to myself. The truth is I wanted everything on a plate or not at all. I was special and odd and anyone that didn't recognise this could f-off.

Christopher, it transpired, was gay. I can't remember how he let it drop but once he'd ascertained that I was not hostile, he invited me to his local gay bar. To my surprise it was in a country hotel. The gay venues I'd been to with Simon, my university flatmate who turned out to be gay, were in central London, where loud music, thick smoke and a catholic sexuality were the order of the day. Women that wanted to dance unmolested, even discreet straight couples attracted to the rawness of a gay club, were welcome. This place, on the other hand, was quiet and roomy and, in a low-key way, gayer. Older, conservatively-dressed men propped up the bar like their straight counterparts in any other pub or hotel.

There wasn't even any music playing, I realised, as Christopher fed coins into a jukebox and punched some numbers. REM's 'Losing My Religion' started up. A guy with a crew-cut in an untucked leaf-green Ralph Lauren shirt came up to us and Christopher introduced me. Ralph Lauren said the place was dead and Christopher said that was how he liked it. If he wanted to be somewhere he couldn't hear people speak and couldn't move it was so packed, he'd have stayed in Manchester. Ralph got the hint and wandered off.

That was when I realised we were on a date. Up until then I'd told myself I was simply being friendly, meeting all sorts as you would expect from a journalist. He'd had a drink with me in a straight pub after our meeting on the cliffs, why shouldn't I now have a drink with him on his turf? It was only fair. Deep down of course I'd known from the beginning, even before he'd told me, that I wasn't interesting enough for his interest in me to be purely platonic.

The evening passed pleasantly enough. There was no dancing, nothing happened that wouldn't occur in an average provincial hotel bar on a Friday night. All the males, which meant everyone, ogled the night away, old geezers told feeble jokes to the young, scantily-dressed bartender and everyone went home, couples together and singles alone.

I saw that the gay subculture was a successful ecosystem, complete with old and young, rich and poor, trendy and square, washed and unwashed. It reminded me of the celebrated communal spirit during the Second World War, when everyone at "home" pulled together. Differences were put aside in the interest of survival. Gays were clearly under attack from society: why else put dark glass in the windows of this and other gay venues, reinforcing the wartime comparison by making it feel like a blackout during an air raid?

Nevertheless in places like this all around the country, gays can feel at home, I told myself, drawing from a pint of manly bitter. I could feel myself getting sentimental about a community that I knew next to nothing about. It wasn't hard, though, to work out why I was touched by the idea of a refuge for outsiders.

I agreed to follow Christopher's car back to his home so that he could give me a tape of Scottish folk music he'd promised to record for me last time we met. Once we were there, I realised I couldn't very well sit in the car while he went into the house, fetched the tape and brought it back out to me. What would I do then: wind down the window, grab the tape and drive off? So I followed him into the house. Once inside, it seemed churlish not to accept his offer of a whiskey after he'd gone to all the trouble of recording a 90-minute tape for me. So I stretched out on the sofa with my feet up in a relaxed, manly way, while Christopher fixed the drinks, put the tape in the deck so we could have a listen, and flopped into the armchair. We made throaty sounds as we sipped our whiskeys, listening to Capercaille sing in Gaelic to the accompaniment of fiddles and penny whistles.

Even though I wasn't gay, it was not the first time I had put myself in a delicate situation like the one I was in now. What, then, was I up to? To start with, I didn't think I was the first straight male in the world to appreciate the overtly flattering attention of a gay man. I'd often observed straight men become macho or exhibit traces of campness, sometimes at the same time, when talking with gays.

So why did we do it? I knew the answer: Because flirting with a gay man was a cheap thrill. We had nothing to lose. Without the throb of our own desire, we could appreciate the subtler pleasure of being desired. There was also the perception that, for a certain kind of gay man, we had the attraction of being "straight-acting" – "real" men. Women were always looking beyond the surface, whereas we could imagine these gay men being more than satisfied with the hunk of hetero male flesh standing before them. In their company our limited prospects and emotional constipation evaporated and we became screen idols. Released from the iron grip of our insecurities, we could imagine that we were enough. No doubt if we could hear what these same guys said about us once we'd gone, we might reconsider quite how much of a hit we'd been.

I drained my whiskey, saying I had to be going. Jumped up, practically snatched the tape out of Christopher's hand and in a few giant strides was at the front door, from the safety of which I turned and said something vague enough to give him some hope of future success. Idols had a responsibility to let their admirers down gently.

I didn't return his calls and we never met again. In many ways my time down in Cornwall, apparently full of drama and anticipation, was one of my loneliest patches. My role of wounded adoptee was, without my realising it, grinding me down. I never went out without a sensitive smile. I smiled sensitively when Alison introduced me as 'my son James', when I really wanted to sneer 'How convenient I'm your son now'. I smiled sensitively when Simon, visiting from London, said he felt most sorry for my mother in all this – when what I really wanted to say was, 'That's because you've never confronted your own mother about your gayness.' And I smiled sensitively when Alison told me that Davy had said (with true generosity, I now see), 'Don't worry about James, Alison, he's a good man,' when I really wanted to howl at her, 'I'm not good. And neither are you. This whole thing's a mess, so let's stop pretending.'

Towards the end of the journalism course we had what Alison has described as one of the worst days in her life and what I considered a long overdue exchange. We went to Helston to try a curry house Alison had heard things about. Storm candles, poppadoms and tinkly music. I cleared my throat: 'When I go back to London I'm not sure I want to keep in touch. It's been hard for me.'

Alison was rattled. She asked me if I regretted finding her.

'No.'

Was it something she'd done?

'Of course not.'

What was the problem then?

It felt like trying to split up with a girlfriend. 'There's no problem,' I said. God forbid I would ever admit to a problem.

Alison let me talk for a bit, before saying, 'If you told your parents it might make things easier.'

She was right, of course, but I certainly wasn't going to admit it to her, the person that had started the problem in the first place. The idea of knowingly causing such a stir at home, of rating my own feelings high enough to think they were worth rocking the foundations of our family over, seemed completely alien. Only my mother's and possibly my sister's feelings were that important. Plus of course I didn't relish the confrontation, the telling them part. Nor did I find the idea of being frozen out of the family exactly appealing. (I might have reflected that I already felt like an outsider and that I didn't have as much to lose as I may like to have thought.)

At some point I remember Alison saying with feeling, 'I want to give you wings.' It was a touching idea, something that a few months ago would have seemed entirely plausible. Now it sounded like a key moment in a romance novel, perhaps one of the Cornish tin-mining sagas Alison's mother had forbidden her children to read because they were historically inaccurate. By wings I took Alison to mean that getting to know her would finally relieve me of the psychological burden of adoption, enabling me at last to attain my full potential, to fly like a bird.

Another interpretation of wings, to fly away with, to flee, did not appear to be what Alison intended. But from where I was sitting, across the table from this emotional woman in her fifties whom I'd somehow become enmeshed with, it was fast becoming my preferred version. In Alison, it seemed, I'd found one more parent to disappoint. That wasn't quite right: I'd found one more concerned witness to my own disappointment. That was why I wanted to flee. And why, deep down, I knew I couldn't. I told myself that meeting Alison had always been about breaking away from my parents, and what was the point in asserting my independence if they didn't even know I'd done it? (It was only later that I realised my less honourable motive for meeting Alison: I wanted to punish my parents, and what was the point of punishing someone who didn't know they were being punished?)

I'd assumed that the root of my insecurity lay in how my parents had dealt with my being adopted. If I could only recreate myself outside of my parents' influence, I could be happy. The problem with this, I can see now, is it assumes a vibrant, creative person waiting only to be set free. It makes my unhappiness seem like a spell cast by unwitting captors.

The truth is that this cruelly imprisoned Renaissance man didn't exist. There was nothing more to me than was already there. That was the awful, sinking, shameful reality that I suspect I knew at some level all along. Much better to lay the blame on my parents when the alternative was starting the long climb of building a career, getting a girlfriend, settling down somewhere for more than six months, relying on friends and being relied on – making a life. That, of course, was the only way I was going to build genuine self-worth, not by magically un-adopting myself. How could meeting Alison, or throwing her in my parents' face, make me feel successful?

If the root of my insecurity wasn't how my parents had dealt with my being adopted, what was the cause? Was I just another spoilt rich boy who hadn't learnt what it meant to achieve something by his own efforts, and/or a victim of being sent away to boarding school aged eight – again sharing the blame with my parents?

Was I deficient as a person? Perhaps, if I hadn't been given up for adoption, I would have ended up blaming Alison and her husband for any dissatisfaction I had with my life.

Or did the very fact of being adopted cause unhappiness, irrespective of how well it was managed by the adoptive parents?

In her groundbreaking book, *The Primal Wound: Understanding the adopted child*, clinical psychologist Nancy Verrier identifies three possible causes for unhappiness in the adoptee. One of these "core issues" is what she calls 'adoption as a concept', the knowing that your birth mother gave you away.

As you grow up, your understanding of what it means to be adopted changes. Up to age seven or eight, I, like any other child, didn't even know what giving birth was, let alone what the opposite of that meant, which was apparently what had happened to me. By my teens, I knew that my birth mother had done what 99.9 per cent of mothers would never dream of doing in their worst nightmare: she'd given her baby away to strangers.

The "concept" of being adopted was confusing. It left you feeling rejected, dirty and, in the end, bad. My "doubling rule" clearly relates to this core issue, in that starting with the premise that you are worse than everyone else leads you to over-compensate. It makes you hyper-vigilant, ready to take offence, or frightened to take part lest you fail and end up feeling rejected, because everything is personal to the adoptee.

Another of Nancy Verrier's core issues goes under the umbrella term "external considerations". One consideration that I can certainly relate to is what she calls 'the insult of secrecy'. Think how powerful secrets seem to children, how much they want to know them and how hard it is to keep them. I was told a Big Secret about myself and then encouraged to forget it – impossible! And as I got older I realised that the secret was really a secret being kept from me.

When I was born, UK law had stated that the adoptive family and birth parents should have no way of contacting each other, in the interest of giving the adoptive family a clean start. In 1976 the law changed, allowing adopted people over the age of 18 access to their birth records. This worried many adoptive parents at the time, mine included, who were concerned that the introduction of birth parents could upset their family unit, not to mention the unfairness of changing the rules halfway through. Of course, the change in law did not affect me at the time; I was ten in 1976 and knew nothing about it. As an adopted child I was simply supposed to feel grateful for the secrecy, as without it I may never have had the chance of a loving two-parent family.

I was expected to trust the judgement of my elders and betters, whereby ensuring I forever remained an adopted child. After all, as Betty Jean Lifton points out on the first page of her moving autobiography, *Twice Born: Memoirs of an adopted daughter*, 'Who has ever heard of an adopted adult?' (The title of this book is, I think, a stroke of genius.)

Another closely linked external consideration referred to by Nancy Verrier is 'a lack of genealogical history'. For years I would have dismissed this as being the obsession of aristocrats and their imitators. What business did I, who spent his time drinking and thinking about sex, have in pretending to be concerned with family trees?

I now believe this to be a very real source of unhappiness. I feel the same hollowness today as twenty years ago whenever anyone observes – probably less often than would normally happen, out of sensitivity to me – that Rachel must have got this or that trait from her mother or father or maternal great aunt. Now she has a young son, the comparisons have four generations to slide back and forth between. Occasionally someone might say I have my father's eyebrows, which only makes matters more awkward. Partly, I admit, this is because Dad's eyebrows are only a twig or two less overgrown than Dennis Healy's.

But it was at public school, where I went from age 13 to 17, that I felt my lack of genealogical history most acutely, although I would not have worded it in quite that way. My father and all his friends had been to public school. It was where you got "character". This I, like many before and after me, confused with *becoming* a character. And when it came to charm, confidence and seemingly effortless success, I needed to look no further than the son of one of my father's best friends.

Steve Decker – two years above me at Cranford – was The Man. I can remember going to a New Year's Eve party thrown by him at his home, while his parents celebrated with my parents and other friends at another venue. Steve was in banana-yellow trousers that night. Through the homemade disco lights, I watched him rub one of his thighs between a girl's legs as he pressed her against the wall and snogged her. I must have been around 14 and it felt like I had a backstage pass to watch God in action. There was no need to take notes as every movement and expression became instantly seared on my mind.

Steve was a character. He made everyone laugh just by opening his mouth. You laughed because you felt so happy to be in his orbit. To be fair, he wasn't bad at repartee. You felt he recycled the same stuff ten times over but so did Oscar Wilde. My greatest moment was when, a few years after the New Year's Eve party, Steve's older sister told me I was like Steve.

Like Steve – what did she mean, exactly?

I had the same way with words, she said.

I could have put my thigh between her legs and snogged her there and then. If I couldn't be Steve, I could be like him. The thing was, I passed – as transvestites say once they've fooled strangers into believing they are the opposite sex. My parents had always treated me as their own, as if I were their biological son. With Steve as my inspiration, I could sense a way to live up to that standard.

I knew I was a fraud, of course. I knew the frightened, needy, calculating baby-turned-boy – the adopted child inside – wouldn't go away. But if I came across as a character, that was good enough for me.

The most controversial aspect of Nancy Verrier's book is her third and final core issue: the assertion that a baby suffers a 'primal wound' when given away by its birth mother. The argument goes that I would have bonded with

Alison in utero, and also during the first ten days of my life, when, through returning my gaze, breastfeeding me, cuddling me and talking to me, she would have provided a bridge between inside and outside the womb. To have that bridge suddenly destroyed must have been a traumatic event, which, on an unconscious level, I would never forget. Fear of abandonment would dominate my life from then on.

In her clinical work, Nancy Verrier claims to have observed similar issues with people who were placed in incubators at birth, even though they were reunited with their mothers once the danger was over. In this regard, I had an advantage over an "incubator baby" in that I'd experienced ten days with Alison before being separated.

The primal wound is impossible to prove scientifically since it occurs at a preverbal time in a person's life. I suppose you could measure the baby's brain activity for signs of increased anxiety after separation, but maybe it was cold, hungry, or wishing it were back in the womb? I believe, however, that my experience of arriving at prep school, the feeling of déjà vu on realising I had been abandoned there, would seem to support the case for the existence of such a wound.

But am I not trying to have it both ways? Either I can't remember being with my birth mother and therefore the primal wound is conjecture, or I can remember being with her, even if it is just a trace of her smell, and therefore the primal wound very likely exists in some form. But to say the primal wound is the result of an unforgettable experience and then be unable to remember it, would appear to be disingenuous.

This is my reply: is it possible to know you are missing something without knowing what it is?

It seems to me that if the primal wound exists, it is experienced by the adoptee as something like a footprint in the sand. The existence of a hole indicates that a foot once stood there. Separation from the birth mother is felt in terms of the emptiness left behind. But soon enough the footprint is filled by the make-believe of adopted life. The first words an adopted child, like any other child, learns to say are "Ma" and "Da". He creates the make-believe as fervently as the faces staring down at him. And soon the only identifiable link to the birth mother is the instinct to make-believe, which provides the foundation of his being. Perhaps the primal wound is really the primal pretending.

An artist friend of mine who is also adopted has recently started seeing a counsellor specialising in adoption issues. He told me that the first thing he said to her was 'I don't feel like a real person.'

'Snap,' I replied, thinking, 'That'll be primal pretending.' From the moment your birth mother gives you away you start performing for your supper. The only problem is that when you try to stop performing there is nobody left; there is no real "you" to return to when the curtain falls. There are, however, two causes for optimism. One is that there is in fact a "you" who knew a time before primal pretending: the week-old baby. It may be possible to feel some tenderness for him. The other cause for hope is that when an actor is performing he or she is a real person, even if they don't much like the roles they are playing.

I find it impossible to say where one core issue begins and another ends. When, on first entering my dormitory at Barton, I saw the check rug that Mummy had chosen for me at the school outfitters magically laid on a bed, was I feeling the 'insult of secrecy', was I 'conceptually' terrified that I was being punished for being adopted, or was I re-experiencing the trauma of being given away by Alison?

One final thought on the theory behind what it means to be adopted: could the three core issues correspond to Freud's developmental stages of a child? The oral phase (from birth to two years old), which is concerned with the fulfilment of basic needs, corresponds to when the adopted child experiences the primal wound. If a birth mother's love and attention are basic needs, then adoption ensures they are unmet.

The anal phase (from two to four years old), when the child discovers his power as an autonomous individual, corresponds to the moment when the adopted child first becomes aware of the concept of adoption – if, like me, you were told from the earliest possible moment. Believing you are innately defective does not help build self-confidence.

The Oedipal phase (from four to five years old), when the child is concerned with his roles in the family, corresponds to the adopted child's understanding of the wider implications of being adopted, such as his lack of genealogical history.

Does any of this theory matter in the end?

Well, it is at least reassuring for the adoptee to know that their feelings of guilt and shame are man-made, rather than having fallen onto them from out of the sky.

*   *   *

I decided to tell my mother before my father. Perhaps I felt one person at a time would be more manageable. The party line, I felt, would be that I was troublemaking. Whatever defence I might come up with (I wasn't trying to hurt anyone; it was my right to find my origins; any "trouble" surely belonged to us all), I certainly felt like the guilty one. Outnumbered as well as guilty, I would be even more likely to accede to all concessions, explicit or implied. Not that I was exactly clear what my parents might make me promise. Never to see Alison again, would make them appear paranoid. Adhere to strict visiting rights, perhaps one weekend every six months, might seem overly prescriptive. Choose between her and them, would be taking brinkmanship to a callous, even wicked extreme.

This uncertainty even in the face of logic is, I believe, an everyday part of being adopted. Growing up, I knew my parents would never give me away like my biological mother had done. I knew this, but that didn't stop me fearing it could happen. My intellect told me my parents had never given me reason to imagine I was anything but a permanent member of the family; my emotions told me nothing to do with humans was certain. If you never trusted anyone completely, you could never be completely disappointed. In this way, I suppose, I kept myself safe from the effects of being given away again. But the cost was provisionality, holding back a fraction, never completely letting down my guard.

We were walking along the harbour towpath at Winbourne when I said, 'I've got something important to tell you'. There would have been dinghies and small keel boats sailing towards the start line. I know it was a warm day, as we sat down on a bench, facing the mud and sea. I can picture seagulls, the swoosh of foaming waves, an occasional murmur of conversation travelling across the water from a boat. Afterwards, Mummy told me she thought I was going to say I had Aids or something equally terrible, such was my solemnity.

'I've met my biological mother,' I said. Met, not found, and biological, not birth or natural, the words handpicked to downplay Alison's importance. Instantly I knew from her face – just as I'd known from Lorna's on the cliff path – that everything would be all right. My announcement had not been the flick of the switch to commence nuclear war.

Once the threat of tears had receded from my eyes, though not from Mummy's, I decided to continue by saying that Alison was large, my mother having a slender build.

A magnanimous smile fought with the tears.

I told Mummy about the pub, describing a somewhat eccentric, parochial set-up – to contrast favourably with my parents' more cosmopolitan, upscale lifestyle. I went through the extraordinary story of our meeting, from encountering the old lady at the crossroads, to overhearing Lorna tell the guard at the tin mine that her mother was a local historian, finally to driving to meet Alison at Lorna's home and no one coming to the door – that last point showing a reassuring lapse in judgement on Alison's part.

Looking back, I can see that each idiosyncrasy I ascribed to Alison happened to match one of my own shortcomings, as seen through my mother's eyes. Without realising it, I was the one negotiating concessions. My terms were that my vagueness, earnestness and at times foolishness could now officially be allocated to Alison. The Mulholland name would forever be cleared of any taint from my less favourable character traits. In return, I need not feel guilty for what I'd done, for betraying my adoptive parents.

Growing up, Mummy had always seemed larger than life. If she were happy, we were happy. If she were angry, we were frightened. The only person that could on occasion outmanoeuvre her was my sister, whose sobbing could reach an intensity that demanded everyone else's feelings be put to one side at least for the duration. When I thought about my mother, I would picture her without borders, filling the entire space of my mind's eye. Her big smile, infectious laugh and easy banter – often of a 'lavatorial nature', to use her phrase – provided the campfire around which the rest of us warmed our souls.

But to this day I can also remember the veins in her neck flexing as she shouted at me, at Dad, at (less often) Rachel. The dynamic was as follows: I would do something to annoy my mother, usually not help around the house, she would shout at me, I'd – occasionally – shout back or more often skulk off, Mummy would shout at Dad for not 'doing something', Rachel would come to me in tears, begging me to say I was sorry and do whatever Mummy wanted me to do 'because otherwise she'll keep shouting at

Daddy', and I would go and apologise and offer to do whatever it was I hadn't done, but be unable to do it because Mummy had already done it herself by then.

As time passed, my image of my mother contracted, so that by the time I was sitting beside her on the towpath bench in Winbourne, telling her about Alison, she still seemed larger than life but there was space around her; she had moved in my mind's eye from extreme close-up to close-up. Her feelings were still bigger than mine, but not necessarily more important.

I can see her, turned as far as possible to face me, her body quite still. She's more generous towards Alison than I anticipated. She wants to know how it was for me meeting my – I think she actually uses the word mother without a birth prefix and without undertow. It feels like she's putting herself in Alison's shoes and even, a novel idea for me to consider, in my shoes. In fact the nearest she comes to negotiating a concession is when she says, 'Just as long as you don't go and live in Cornwall,' which I take to mean, Please don't let it seem as if we're no longer number one.

It might also be a warning against hoping for too much from Alison.

I can tell the resentment I have harboured against my mother by the fact that it is only now, in the final draft of this book – eight years after the event – that I can write the one missing sentence from my account of this episode. Sitting with my mother on that thin wooden bench, I knew I loved her. In her unexpected fragility, I saw the person who had brought me up. I felt the gratitude that I had been fighting against for as long as I could remember.

* * *

Recalling our towpath conversation some time later, Mummy said, 'I couldn't help thinking people watching us must wonder who that old lady was, sitting with that young man.' As with a number of my mother's comments, you knew something was up when she said it but because of the casual delivery you let it slide, telling yourself you must have misunderstood it, failed to grasp the context, or be over-reacting. It was only later as the words replayed in my head that I realised I'd been niggled. But by then it seemed like it was too late, although of course it never is too late to ask someone what they meant by something. It felt too late because I wanted to avoid the confrontation, during which not only was I unlikely to get any closer to understanding the first curve ball but in all probability I'd receive another one for good measure. I knew from experience that if I decided to go ahead and question her after the event about something she'd said, her response would form around two principles: 1. She couldn't remember the exact words she'd used last week/month/year (so you were very likely misquoting her); and 2. You shouldn't read into things so much (in other words, Don't impose your mixed-up ideas on me!).

I've got my theories about this particular comment of my mother's. Taken literally, 'I couldn't help thinking people watching us must wonder who that old lady was, sitting with that young man,' could be a way of expressing the alienation she felt during the original conversation on the towpath. Perhaps it was sufficiently unsettling to make her fantasise that she was an onlooker, not personally involved. It might also have been a subconscious attempt to start seeing me as a man rather than just her son, as operating outside as well as inside the family. This in turn may have been an attempt to empathise with Alison, who must experience me in a similarly confusing way. Or it may simply have been her way of telling me how intense she'd found the conversation, and how unusual – how unlike anything we'd ever had before, and therefore how unlike her experience of a mother–son interaction. After all, how often did a mother and son question the very nature of their connection to each other?

My knee-jerk interpretation was, true to form, to see the comment as a put-down. Mummy had been accusing me of doing an unnatural act, of poisoning our relationship to such an extent that we no longer looked like a mother and son, but rather an "old lady" and a "young man".

For me, the worst part about telling Mummy about Alison had been from the moment I asked her if she wanted to go on a walk along the towpath, to the moment I announced, 'I've got something important to tell you.' My stomach had floated around my body like an astronaut while my legs somehow transported me to the bench. From then on, from when I realised it would be all right and my worst, most illogical fears were groundless, I might almost go so far as to say I enjoyed myself. It was fun being in control. I was still the same little boy who wanted his mother's attention, only this time I'd got it by being grown-up rather than showing off.

We found Dad in their bedroom when we returned, and his first words after I told him were, 'We always thought you would,' followed by, 'I'm only surprised it took you so long!'

What about when you said, 'We hope you'll never try to find them'? I thought. I looked at my mother, who seemed to be in agreement with Dad. Were they changing their tune now they saw it was too late? But one look in Dad's eyes told me he was in earnest. Maybe – here was quite a thought – maybe they'd told me that in order to reassure me that they wanted me all to themselves. After all, what kind of parents willingly shared the title of mother or father with someone else? Was it not children, more than parents, who needed the proof of possessive love? 'I remember you once saying to me,' I said, 'you hoped I'd never try to find them. It was when we were sitting in the lounge –' I petered out. What mattered was what they felt now, not what I thought they'd thought five years ago.

'I don't think we'd have said that,' Dad said or words to

that effect.

I can only remember two other things from the conversation in my parents' bedroom in Winbourne, with a view over the harbour and green lawns stretching up to the mansions on the far shore. One was their saying the reason they'd encouraged me so much at swimming was they'd known through the adoption association that my biological father had been an international water-polo player. I could picture myself pounding lengths at the Leatherhead Leisure Centre while Mr Parlour, the personal coach they'd retained for me, crouched at one end with his stopwatch. I still had that tracksuit top sagging with badges.

It was a touching thought, their seeing the positive side to my genes, admiring my DNA. At prep school sports day I'd finished the 4x4 individual medley, described over the tannoy as the most demanding of all events, half a length ahead of the competition, sprung out of the water and sat coolly on the side of the pool, watching the other boys finish. My parents had been proud of me, and I sensed with a boyish thrill they were proud of me now.

The only other item I can remember from that conversation was my mother saying, 'One day, when you're ready, we'd really like to meet her.'

My reply, needless to say, was vague, though on balance one might have interpreted it to be in the affirmative.

5
Loneliness

Fagging, the public school practice of junior boys acting as unpaid, sometimes abused servants of senior boys, had vanished by the time of my arrival at Cranford in 1980. If Margaret Thatcher had begun freeing Britain from the grip of union fag-masters, it was only right for her followers to move with the times too. But parents sending their sons and daughters to public school today would find the institution as different from when I was there, as I would have found it from my father's day.

Cranford in the 21st century has girls, living in what can only be described as a hotel sited on a leafy plot at one end of the 1st XV rugby pitch. When I last spoke to one of my godfathers, who is a governor of the school, he said everyone was agreed that the introduction of girls (shortly after my departure) had had a 'civilising effect'.

I was pleased to hear it, and envious. The modernisation of practices and facilities that all public schools have embraced, or been forced to endure, since my glory days can only be a good thing overall. Admittedly they've moved even further from their traditional purpose, which was first and foremost to produce a sound chap, someone who could go out to India and administer a district without allowing emotions to cloud judgement. But instead they now offer first class teaching, a fabulous array of extra-curricular activities and a friendly atmosphere where bullying has been slashed to a minimum. If this shift means students today lack an old-school sense of civic duty, it's a worthwhile sacrifice.

Trevor Burman, the headmaster of my prep school, had advised my parents to keep me at Barton House an extra term because I needed more time to 'mature' before moving on to public school. As if all the other boys in my year starting at Cranford in September would be well rounded and socially mature! He of sea and sand, Mr Pastel Shades Burman, was no doubt acting honourably, believing he should not allow his more vulnerable chicks to leave downy Barton until they were ready to fend for themselves in the public school snake pit. Naturally my parents followed his advice; like good public school boy and girl they did not allow emotions to cloud their judgement. Or was it the other way round: were they trying so hard to be balanced, they let emotions walk all over their judgement?

What happened, of course, was that by the time I arrived at Cranford everyone else had had a term to make friends and broker alliances. Staying on at Barton had only made certain I would actually be the outsider that I already felt I was. In that sense Burman *et al* had at least ensured that when I finally made my entrance into the Third Form prep room at St Bartholomew's (my house at Cranford) I wouldn't be experiencing anything new.

My father had broken with tradition in putting me down for Cranford rather than Stoke, where he and his two brothers had gone, after, the story goes, my mother had been appalled by the omnipresent whiff of stale milk when accompanying my uncle on a visit to the old school. The other reason was that my father's two best friends – my godfathers – had attended Cranford and, crucially, sent their sons there. My father believed that Cranford, with its no nonsense Midlands location, state of the art workshops and strong rugby tradition, together with thoroughly decent alumni, was more suitable than Stoke or my mother's first choice, Eton, destination of aristocrats and "show offs", to use my father's label.

My first contact with Cranford School and St Bartholomew's House had come during a visit Dad, Mummy and I had taken during an exeat from Barton. We had arranged to be shown around the school by one of my godfathers and his wife, who had three of their four sons currently there. First stop was a visit to the Spar, where Auntie Rosemary bought dried curry meals and packets of biscuits for 'the boys'. While she dropped off a parcel for their youngest, Sammy, who was at the small prep school attached to Cranford, Uncle Kenneth showed us the cloisters, an ancient sand-coloured building with a massive courtyard. Voices carried to us through open windows where lessons were obviously taking place; a burst of collective laughter crackled from somewhere on the first floor. I hoped no one would look out, see us standing there in the middle of the courtyard and call out something. We must look rather keen, I remember thinking.

After reuniting with Auntie Rosemary, we continued the tour, taking in the town itself, where a chemist and sweet shop were pointed out to me, then School House – peered at through a tall grey stone arch; the science block, low, concrete and with an incongruous orange roof; and the state of the art workshops, where their second son Martin had renovated a sports car! Finally, we came to St Bartholomew's, known as St B, a blackened, ivy-cloaked Georgian residence surrounded by a stone wall. Uncle Kenneth told me that he'd been there, his 'first', George, had been there, his 'second and third', Martin and Paul, were there now, and his 'youngest', Sammy, would be going next year. It was only once he'd got to Sammy that I breathed a sigh of relief, realising he was referring to the ages of his sons and not his order of preference.

Uncle Kenneth told Dad that St B was ideally situated midway between the town and playing fields. Confidently shouldering open the front door, he led us to meet the housemaster in his study. We would have sat on one of the six or seven faded armchairs and sofas that helped give this nominally large room a cramped, oxygen-depleted feel. The other influence was Mr Thoms himself, but I hadn't had this robotic, tradition-bound man as my tutor for five years yet to know that about him. In the car going home, Dad would say that it had been meeting Mr Thoms – who thankfully took no notice of me, but seemed grave despite laughing at Uncle Kenneth's jokes – that had finally sold St B to him. Lore has it my name was put down there and then.

As we were being shown out of the study, Uncle Kenneth asked Mr Thoms ('out of courtesy,' he later explained to us) if he would mind if we dropped off some rations for Paul. Everyone thanked Mr Thoms for his 'kindness' when he said we could, even though it seemed to me it was we who were doing Paul the favour, regarding the biscuits if not the dried curries. I can remember the corridor, which had notices pinned everywhere, being so quiet you could hear the different sounds our shoes made on the stone floor.

At the end we turned left and went down a narrower corridor with doors on either side. Uncle Kenneth pushed open one and we entered a small room with two desks, each with three shelves on top, giving the units a top heavy, unstable look. Every available surface was covered in different coloured exercise books, new text books coated in plastic and old ones with peeling spines, trainers, tennis rackets, games socks, and mugs with cold coffee at the bottom. What a mess! I thought but I didn't say anything.

Uncle Kenneth said to me it might be quiet now but wait until lessons ended, it would be a madhouse!

I smiled, picturing Paul, whom I hardly knew, and thirty boys like him all foaming at the mouth, wailing and banging their heads against the walls. Auntie Rosemary was tutting at a photo of a girl in a bikini stuck on Paul's desk. Uncle Kenneth told her to leave it there, everyone had them. My parents chuckled knowingly. I was picturing a wedge of 16-year-old boys bulldozing through the main entrance, which I could see through Paul's study window. We didn't want to be around when that happened.

I can't remember anything else about the trip except that at some point we drove out of town to a field behind a pub, where Uncle Kenneth and Auntie Rosemary had a caravan. I can imagine my father being genuinely impressed with the setup and my mother cooing while no doubt thinking, *That's not for us, thank you very much.* For my part, it seemed cosy and inviting and a further sign that Cranford would be an extension of home, rather than a separate world like Barton.

Uncle Kenneth was "in charge" of boiling water on the gas stove and we had tea or coffee, sitting on deckchairs in ankle-deep grass. Mummy sighed, saying what bliss it was to be off her feet after a day tearing around.

Uncle Kenneth said the landlord never normally let the grass get this long, his eyes fixed on a row of bulging bin-bags topped by haloes of flies along the back wall of the pub.

Auntie Rosemary said the pub was normally good at making sure the rubbish was removed first thing in the morning, which, I could tell, made Mummy want to burst out laughing but she managed to control herself.

Dad would have said something like, 'They must've had a big night!' allowing the men to laugh with their deep voices, and Auntie Rosemary to tut at what rascals they were.

I was left in no doubt we were socially superior to them, and that by extension I would be even more successful at Cranford than their sons. If Martin could renovate a sports car, I would surely be making an aeroplane from scratch.

Driving away in the late afternoon, Mummy and I turned our heads to look at the sun shining on the steeple of the school chapel, which Uncle Kenneth had said boasted an award-winning stained glass window. Cranford seemed big in every way. And the people – the voices drifting out of windows into the huge cloisters, Uncle Kenneth and Auntie Rosemary in their caravan, even Thoms with his fake laugh – seemed small. At Barton, Burman and all the other staff towered over everything; there was nowhere you could be that Fred couldn't find you – well, almost nowhere. Whereas you felt dwarfed by Cranford and, paradoxically, less exposed, safer somehow. I won't say I looked forward to going to Cranford; aged eleven I rarely looked ahead more than a day, let alone two years. But I have no doubt I quizzed my parents for much of the drive home about rugby, state of the art workshops and all the Cranfordians, old and current, that they knew.

*   *   *

If this were a film I would walk into the Third Form prep room at St B, the runt arriving a term late (but how mature!), and everyone would turn to look at me in silence. But I don't remember that happening. What I recall is sitting at my desk, taking in the scene while making sure I didn't catch anyone's eye. The room went on forever. Tall sash windows ran along one side looking onto a lawn the size of a rugby pitch. It was like ten of Paul's studies joined end to end. Books, tapes, clothes, Pot Noodle cartons and plates with congealing food on them formed a landscape of possessions as far as the eye could see. Battered tuck boxes – a sure sign that their owners had come from prep, not day school – teetered on the top shelves of most desks, which seemed to be positioned in groups like clumps of giant mushrooms. Steve Wright would have been doing his Mr Angry voice on the radio or playing a song. I can picture a shrimp of a boy with a pudding bowl haircut lobbing objects over the top of his desk. I can hear them land, cheers rise up, but still there is no reaction from the recipient the other side. Two boys lean back on chairs, talking. Others read comics or stare into space.

My desk was nearest the door with an empty one beside me, just as I'd had an empty bed beside me in the dormitory the night before. A boy called Daniel Kim, it seemed, was not only starting in January like me but had also managed to arrive late for the beginning of term. And if that wasn't bad enough, before he'd even got here the two of us had been linked in a homosexual pact.

The night before – my first night at Cranford – I'd got up to have a pee and must have got back into Daniel Kim's empty bed by mistake. By the time we went down for breakfast I'd been named Norman and poor Daniel Kim Jeremy, after the politician Jeremy Thorpe and his lover Norman Scott, protagonists in a recent sex scandal. The name never stuck for Daniel Kim, because from the moment he arrived and it became apparent he was part-Asian (his father was Korean), he naturally had to be called Chinky, Nippon, Slant Eyes or Ah-so. Norman lasted for a while but because I didn't react – perhaps believing I deserved the name! – it was soon replaced by Proboscis, after my larger than average nose, or Big Ass, the name I liked least.

There was a boy in St B a year above me, reasonably popular on account of sporting success, who was called Manuel after the character in *Fawlty Towers*. The reason for this nickname was that he once confided in a friend that he was adopted, and the joke was that his father could therefore be anyone, even an idiotic Spanish waiter. Oddly, it never crossed my mind that Uncle Kenneth and Auntie

129

Rosemary's "youngest", Sammy, might know – perhaps because he was so meek – so I never seriously worried about my big secret, my centre of shame, getting out. Nonetheless it was a reminder of my vulnerability, and made Proboscis or Norman seem complimentary by comparison.

The Third Form scholars didn't appear to have nicknames, living on another planet. Everyone else had been given one the previous term based on their most obvious vulnerability; there was Gibbon (long arms), Tonky (big nose), Tiny (penis), Brick (thick), Chicken Neck (deformed spine) and so on. Someone called Tomato Face had been so badly bullied in the winter term that after a week back he rang home and called it a day. He packed his stuff and was apparently collected while we were in lessons, but just to be sure a group of Third-formers howled 'Tomato Face!' at any car with a boy and adult inside seen driving past the prep room as we waited for the lunch bell.

Mike Harris was a Third-former whose legend lived on even though he hadn't returned for the spring term. Tomato Face's chief tormentor, Mike had put a dead vole in his bed, covered his desk in ketchup and taken his bike for a spin before leaving it on top of a wall for all to see. *R.I.P. Mike Harris* could be found carved into desks, on the inside of bog doors and even on a chapel pew. Everyone missed Mike, they said. The guy was an outlaw!

Finally there was Timothy Beasley. He liked classical music and butterflies. He was, to use the preferred term, a drop out. He had no friends. About the nicest thing anyone called him was Carrot Top, after his hair. But when the prep room wanted to insult him the name of choice was Thle. He had a slight lisp and most likely, sometime in the winter term, in the salad days before my arrival, he must have pronounced the end of his surname rather too precisely, emphasising that lisp. I can hear and see Tiny quietly repeating, 'Thle, Thle, Thle,' and others joining in until the whole prep room vibrated with his name.

'Thle, Thle, Thle,' Thle heard, sitting at his island-desk. 'Go join Tomato Face . . . No friends . . . Thle, Thle, Thle.' But, for better or worse, Timothy Beasley was made of sterner stuff than Tomato Face. He lasted all five years and I honestly don't think he had a single friend in all that time apart from his butterfly books and recordings of Schubert.

I can clearly remember Chinky, a nice guy deep down but a follower, putting his face inches from Thle's and shouting, 'Drop out – drop out – drop out. No friends – no friends – *no friends.*' It was a performance that even Tiny might have been surprised by. In another environment Chinky's outburst may have signalled the simultaneous height and decline of Thle-baiting, in the same way that Caligula's antics marked the beginning of the end for the Roman Empire. Here was Thle-baiting in its full vulgarity for all to see. There was no finesse, no new variation, nothing to amuse. Anyone who had ever shouted Thle would know that they were in some way part of this crescendo of cowardice. But in the prep room such realisations went unobserved. It would be like asking the Roman mob if they'd had enough of gladiatorial combat. Thle was remorselessly bullied for his entire time in the prep room, and largely ignored from then on.

How far did I take part in this bullying? Moralists would say I was guilty because I was there and let it happen, whether or not I actively took part. Hand on heart, I don't remember chanting Thle or even insulting him to his face and if that sounds like a politician's answer, it's the best I can do. In a way a more interesting question is why I didn't take part in the Thle chorus if it were such a popular activity. Did I get a thrill imagining I was too good to be involved, too moral? Possibly, but more likely I simply didn't feel I belonged enough to join in. Although I would never have admitted it to myself, let alone to the Third

Form prep room, deep down I empathised with Thle. He was on the outside, what I was on the inside – a runt. But that didn't mean I was about to be foolish enough to stick up for him even for a second.

I showed what I was made of in the Fourth Form, however, when Daniel Kim and I were the only two put in a dormitory with the new Third-formers. Lying in bed after lights out, the two of us would loudly suck snot from our noses, gargle it ominously and then launch green frothy "gobs" in soaring arcs across the room. I was prop and Daniel was flanker in the junior colts rugby team. If a gob hit someone on the face they'd complain, but no one did anything about it. I don't remember continuing this diversion for that long so I imagine we must have got bored.

The *Owzat* die that my father had given me, saying he'd played it with friends when he was at public school, was clearly part of another world. As was his old boy network of jolly Uncle Kenneth and sporty Uncle Peter. And the nicknames for his school friends, such as Taffy – because, that's right, the guy was Welsh – seemed to be from a *Boy's Own* manual. But there was no way I could begin to tell Dad what Cranford in the 1980s was really like. I would have felt like I'd personally failed him, as if I'd somehow managed to dirty what had once been a shining institution.

I never wondered if his school days had really been so different from mine, if they'd been as innocent and friendly and sexually unsullied as he implied. It never crossed my mind that Dad could have been gobbed on by an older boy for months on end, or have taken part in trapping some wretch in a corner of the prep room while screaming brutally personal insults at him. Maybe none of these things ever happened and his school days were exactly as he made them seem. That was certainly what I believed at the time, and I have heard nothing from Dad since, despite asking him several open questions, to contradict this version.

But you had to deal with how things were, not how you thought they should be. I would have to approach my integration into Third Form society at St B like a pro. I was a pro, after all; a graduate in the art of coping. I'd probably been doing it since entering foster care, aged ten days. Certainly I became accomplished soon after arriving at Barton, lying in my own cold pee night after night without saying a word. The prep room didn't really scare me. You just had to stay alert and know who to flatter, while giving every appearance of looking like an innocent abroad, ignorant of the games people played to get ahead.

Once a week there was a space in the timetable when we were meant to do something semi-supervised in our houses and, arriving a term late, I appeared to have been left out of the loop. For at least a term I lay on my bed listening to my Walkman, plotting whom to be friends with, how to make them like me, and reviewing my strategy in the light of events that week. I decided I wanted to be part of the popular set, in other words the loud set. At the set's core were three boys, Dave (Tiny), Ian and Will, who had been at the same prep school, a clear advantage from the start.

I could see that the best way to avoid being cut by Dave's sharp tongue was to appear popular. Dave only went for low risk, easy kills. In this way he created a no-win situation, where you were picked on for not being popular and the only way to stop being picked on was to be popular!

Ian, the cute one, the pure one, the one whose mother believed in him – you could always tell – seemed to have too much integrity to be moved in on. You had to let Ian choose you.

So it would have to be Will, a.k.a. Dago on account of his swarthy complexion. Will – tall, handsome and good at sports – was destined for success, at least within the milieu of Cranford. I could see myself at his side. I was in the squash team, he was in the hockey team. He'd been in the under 14 rugby team last term (while I was "maturing" at Barton); nothing would stop me joining him in the junior colts next year.

The plotting worked! At the end of our first year everyone moved out of the Third Form prep room into five or six-man studies and I was accepted into, even co-designed, the popular study – although by then we were possibly the only ones who saw ourselves in that light. One of the first things Will and I did was buy a second-hand television and smuggle it into the study. We housed it under a table and protected it from prying eyes with a drape. While everyone waited for everyone else to fall asleep so they could give their chap a tug, we – the "popular" set – would sneak out of the dormitory to watch *Match of the Day* or a late night film that looked as if it might have nudity in it.

The next year we moved into three-man studies in the same corridor as the one Paul, my godfather's son, had had when I'd visited with my parents all that time ago. By now Will and I were best mates and we chose Neil, a down-to-earth Yorkshireman, to accompany us. I mention this because it forms the prelude to a devastating turn of events.

In the Upper Sixth we moved into bedsits. Those at the top of the list – school prefects, followed by house prefects by age, then everyone else by age – got first refusal of the limited number of one-man rooms. Will, a school prefect, and Neil, the oldest in the year, both took one-mans, leaving me . . . It was humiliating, frightening. I can remember crying openly in our study, Will seated at his desk, me standing in the doorway, as he told me he would not consider sharing a two-man with me. (Years later he admitted regretting the decision but making it because 'I thought it's what Dad would've done'.)

It is a measure of how upset I was that I was unable to hide my true feelings in front of Will. I did not try to dissuade him, however, perhaps because I could see there was no chance of success, but also because deep down his decision made sense to me. Like my biological mother and parents before him, Will had finally seen the truth and decided to give me away. I had had a good run but after four years the deception that I was, I almost want to say "real", that I was enough had finally caught up with me.

I was, I knew, in a helpless situation: everyone who could see they were going to be in a two-man had already paired off. Everyone except a disconcerting, pasty creature named Ted Clarke, who played no sports, was a wiz at maths and had no real friends – but had somehow avoided, possibly through an aloof independence, being labelled a dropout. And Timothy Beasley, of course, though logic dictates there must have been a fourth lost soul as Timothy had certainly not been made a house prefect and would therefore have had to pair up with someone.

Clarke and I teamed up and then spent a term falling out, until we barely acknowledged each other and the time came for us to part company. Timothy's roommate must have agreed to take Clarke, and Timothy moved in with me. Those hours lying on my bed, listening to my Walkman and plotting, had come to this! I was sharing a bedsit with Thle. But deep down it felt horribly right. My outside now fitted my inside, I looked like how I felt: an outsider, a grinning nobody.

Adoption had caught up with me at last. All pretence that I was part of a line of thoroughbred Old Cranfordians, traceable back through Steve Decker (he of the banana-yellow trousers and magnetic repartee) to my godfathers, was officially over. I had failed to be the biological son of Adrian Mulholland.

The idea, however, was a lot worse than the reality. One grey Midlands Sunday afternoon we sat sipping Lapsang Souchong – Timothy's tea of choice – listening to an audio-book of *The Importance of Being Earnest*, and I was introduced to a wit altogether more sophisticated than Monty Python or Rowan Atkinson. If Timothy was formal, he was also considerate. He brought a feminine softness to the room, although there was nothing effeminate or homosexual about him. In his tolerance of his peers, and the way he remained true to himself, he was perhaps the most powerful, even masculine, of us all. If I have a regret it is that I didn't value his friendship sufficiently; I only offered him companionship behind a bedsit door.

* * *

Cranford wasn't all strangled hope and loneliness – staples of adolescence wherever you grew up, after all. Daniel and I had our first foray into Girls at the age of 13, when we would walk over to the housing estate after army corps on Wednesday afternoons. In our combat gear we were no doubt as readily identifiable as public school gits as if we'd arrived in boaters and blazers.

A 1970s construction, the estate was a maze of winding streets lined with identical semis: red tile roof, double-glazing, low brick wall in front of a small lawn. It was like entering a faraway land, more foreign than St Tropez or Courchevel. *How could people live in houses that were identical to their neighbours?* I thought, without realising that I was "identical", even down to my thoughts, to the stereotypical public schoolboy. I can remember, true to form, being titillated by the idea of there being countless Eliza Dolittles within these homes, waiting for a chance to meet their Freddy.

Daniel was bolder than me. Through his instigation, we had a number of thrilling conversations on the pavement with girls with Midlands accents who (with the benefit of hindsight) made fun of us until they got bored. Once, however, two girls, clearly friends rather than sisters, offered us tea.

We'd got talking in the usual way. Girl 1 asks Daniel

something like, 'Are you Pike, 'en?'

Fortunately Daniel seems to know what she's on about and replies, 'I am. And this is Captain Mannering. So you had better salute him.'

Dad's Army, I realise. I'm about to tuck a pretend stick under my arm and bark an order, when I realise they'll think I'm just Daniel's straight man; Wise to Daniel's Morecambe. I've got to come up with a joke of my own. Because jokes show you're a character. I know this much from watching Steve Decker. 'We're in the SAS,' I say, which I don't think is too bad an effort under pressure.

'Why've you got a wimpy body, 'en?' Girl 2 asks Daniel. 'If you're SAS?'

'Good question,' I say, assuming she chose to address this to Daniel because she's noticed my rugby-enhanced physique. 'Good question,' I say again with a smirk, because Steve Decker does that. The second time round is like an encore.

Daniel sends me a sideways glance. *I thought we were working together?* it says.

It makes me wonder what exactly we are supposed to be working together towards. It seems unlikely we're going to pair off in the street and have snogs. That means we're "getting to know" them, which suits me fine. I don't want my first-ever snog to be in broad daylight (13-year-old talk for *I'm terrified*).

This is when Girl 1 decides to move things on, and asks us if we'd like a cup of tea.

We say, 'Why not?' We stand around outside their gate while they go back into the house, leaving the front door open. At the end of a narrow unlit corridor I can make out a small formica table top and a chair with a coat thrown on it. It feels like a glimpse up a skirt, except I can keep looking.

I can see that view into the house as clearly today as 25 years ago. The open-plan kitchen was in all likelihood not much smaller than my parents' (and had to be more generous than the one my wife and I squeeze into in our London terrace house in an up-and-coming area); but I saw what I wanted to see, which was smallness and cheapness. The thought that kept going through my mind was, *Imagine if that was your life.* I kept swinging between thinking how unbearably claustrophobic it would be, and how wonderfully free – nothing would be expected of you, I imagined with crass ignorance.

Believe it not, I made no connection between this fantasy and the life I could have had if I hadn't been given up for adoption. I didn't think about being adopted unless it was being talked about, which was almost never. I was simply drawn by something forbidden, something unknown, about the glimpse down that corridor.

The girls came out with a mug each, grins on their faces. After both of us had taken a sip, they burst out laughing.

It did taste funny, we admitted.

That, they said, was because they'd put gravy in it!

It might have been then or another time that a bunch of local lads, possibly the Cranford Boot Boys who sprayed their logo around town like cats in the Serengeti, saw us talking to two of "their" girls. What I remember next is a block of youth hurtling towards us, calling out things. Daniel and I ran for it, darted down a side passage and hid behind someone's hedge. We heard them bustle past, telling each other – and us, if we were nearby – they were sick of seeing us around here. If they caught us here again they'd send us to hospital. My heart was pounding painfully against my ribcage. When we were sure they'd gone, we peered around the hedge and ran and ran and ran, not stopping until we reached the yawning, resplendent playing fields of Cranford School.

I had my first date when I was 14. Sophie White was a friend of my sister's best friend, Debs, from when they had all been at the local convent school together. Then Rachel had gone to public school, while Debs and Sophie had moved up the road to the senior school. I must have met Sophie during the previous holidays, although I don't remember the occasion, because I had her, or rather her parents' phone number.

Fortunately Sophie answered when I rang, at a strategic 5pm. I made conversation for a few minutes, as if we spoke most days, and then asked her if she'd like to have lunch at Pizza on the Park on Saturday.

Just like that, she agreed! It was remarkable. I could hardly picture her face. She seemed to know who I was though. What a stud!

When I put down the receiver, Gavin Lemesurier came out of the study opposite the pay phone and said with apparent sincerity something like, 'What a wonderful telephone manner you have, James.'

I thanked him, thinking, Let's hope the next part works out as well, i.e. she turns up. The idea of having a real-life girlfriend was more than I could contemplate at this point. But, but, if Saturday went well . . .

*   *   *

The Fourth Form was going on educational trips that Saturday to places like Cambridge and Stratford-upon-Avon. I don't know how I managed to avoid having my name down on any trip. As a pupil you imagine some teacher would check everyone was down for something, but apparently no one did, because as everyone else boarded coaches, I slunk onto a bus to Peterborough.

Being on the bus was somewhat like visiting the housing estate: you felt the thrill of roughing it but also the fear of normality, of erasure. I was in jeans and trainers, sitting among pensioners and mums with prams. There was nothing to differentiate me from a local lad, even a Cranford Boot Boy – or was there? Flat fields with crops went by, interrupted by the occasional village with a mini-estate on the edge and one shop in the middle.

Finally – Peterborough, a once-small market town "expanded" (flattened) by pouring 50 million tons of concrete on top of it in the 1960s under the New Town initiative. We'd learnt that in human geography. Teens padded along walkways gripping Our Price bags, grownups padded along walkways gripping British Home Stores bags. But looked at logically, if everything and everybody were the same, it had to make getting a girlfriend easier. There was always that disquieting thought about Peterborough residents to mull over, as the King's Cross-bound train pulled out of the station.

London was another planet. The New Romantic phase was in full swing and I went to the Common Market in the King's Road, recommended by an older boy who actually lived in London. Leather, velvet, silk clothes in black and purple hung from row upon row of metal rails. There was lipstick, ear studs, chains – for men or women! It was like being in a Human League video. I almost couldn't believe I was allowed in.

After staring at the clothes in awe for a while, touching their strangeness, I descended into the basement, where there were more clothes as well as a small coffee bar. A punk with a pitch black Mohican was sitting on a stool, stirring a coffee. Talking to him from behind the bar was a girl with piercings in every imaginable place on her face. She looked like a pincushion. I didn't have the guts to plant myself on a stool and order a coffee. Instead I perused a table of leather fingerless gloves, as worn by Marc Almond. There wasn't a size big enough for me. In the footwear area I spied some amazing winkle-pickers in white or black with side-lacing. A girl with pink pixie boots, torn black fishnet stockings and Cindy Lauper-style yellow ribbons in her hair – a mishmash of styles that left me breathless – asked if I wanted anything.

'I'd like some of them,' I said 'in black.'

'They're brilliant, aren't they?'

'Yeah.'

'Joe Jackson had some on . . .'

'I saw that!' Is this love? 'On . . .' Could you say *Top of the Pops* in here?

'*Top of the Pops*. 'Cept he had the white ones. What size?'

I told her. While she went to fetch them I looked at the price: £25. No pudding for Sophie White. I crouched down to inspect the DMs, some of which would come up to your knees – until she came back with my winkle-pickers. The point at the end was so long, there was about three inches of air beyond my toes. They were fantastic. I left them on and put my trainers in the box. They felt a bit wobbly as I went back up the stairs, into daylight. I wished I had the white trousers, purple shirt and asymmetrical haircut as well. Phil Oakey was my hero.

Around a year later – as we sat around the Fifth Form kitchen, making fried egg stacks and bemoaning our fate locked away in a Midlands prison – I would decide I'd had enough of conformity. Using someone's electric razor, I would shave off most of the hair on one side of my head. With the other side as long as the rules permitted, not even Phil could have accused my hair of being symmetrical. To finish off the look, I "sterilised" a compass in boiling water and got Daniel to hold my expectant earlobe, numbed by ice, on the kitchen top and stab a hole through it. I can still hear the sound of tearing flesh today and feel the throb of infection as my lobe swelled up around the stud. I was in the colts rugby team by then and felt my masculinity was assured, allowing me to dip my toe in the "gender bender" culture, as New Romance was called at the time.

But such a statement of tribal allegiance was a year away for the 14-year-old waiting for Sophie White at the entrance of Pizza on the Park.

Leaning casually against a railing, my eyes flicked

between the *NME* I'd bought at Tower Records and my new winkle-pickers with the side-lacing. One day, I told myself, I want to work at a coffee bar in a place like the Common Market. It was truly the summit of my ambition.

'Hi,' said two voices.

I looked up – at Sophie, and Debs. Sophie explained she'd brought Debs along. You didn't say! It was all ruined. She didn't fancy me. She despised me. She'd only accepted so they could have a good laugh at my expense afterwards. But I didn't say anything and in we went, and out came my wallet at the end of the meal. I don't remember if we did anything afterwards. I didn't see Sophie White again, I know that.

*   *   *

Being in the rugby team was key to my self-worth, especially being a prop, probably the most physical position on the field. Dad came to watch every home match and most away matches. When he could, he left the office early and drove up to watch Tuesday afternoon fixtures as well. He would stalk the touchline, just as he did for his local club in Surrey, where he was president, yelling at our forwards to 'Heave!' in scrums and mauls, at our backs to 'Pass the ball!' and at the opposition to 'Get on-side!' and 'Stop blocking the ball!'

Once, the referee, an old-school teacher who wore baggy knee-length shorts like Stanley Matthews, went up to Dad on the touchline and asked him to leave. No one was exactly sure what Dad had done wrong. Probably making too much noise and intimidating the opposition, which was the whole point! Possibly using bad language.

In the changing room after the match, however, everyone was agreed on one thing. It was the first time any of us had heard of a spectator being sent off! They all thought it was hilarious. I thought it was embarrassing, of course, but also touching. At least Dad got involved. He knew the names of most of the players, what their strengths and weaknesses were. He wanted us to win more than we did.

In Dad's book, if you were a rugby player, you were a good bloke. It was as simple as that. There were some rough diamonds at my father's club, a builder called Hemmings who was, in my father's words, 'essentially a thug', but when push came to shove, they were all decent chaps. Rugby did that to you. It taught you to work in a team. It taught you to get on with other men. It overrode class boundaries. And I would agree with all that, if without my father's religious fervour.

There was one place, however, where class boundaries within rugby remained rock solid: the West Stand car park at Twickenham. I first went there when I was about ten or eleven to watch England play Scotland in what was then the Five Nations Championship. Dad, Mummy, my friend James (the one who'd charmed his way into my parents' car at Barton) and I arrived at around 10:30am, three-and-a-half hours before kick-off in order to secure our usual spot in the car park. My two godfathers would have arrived at about the same time, and soon enough three car boots had been opened up and their contents arranged on fold-out tables. It was a well-oiled machine: Dad, Uncle Kenneth and Uncle Peter divided up who brought which drinks, while Mummy, Auntie Rosemary and Auntie Wendy took care of the food side.

In those days, before Dad retired, it was my mother's job to drive home, allowing Dad the opportunity to have a good booze-up with his rugby pals. Everyone (who was anyone) knew where to find us and people dropped by for a jar before going back to their own or another's car. As a rule it was ale for the men, G'n'T for wives. Men wore suede coats with the sheepskin collar turned up, wives hugged long cashmere overcoats with matching scarves and hats. Conversation had a confident braying quality punctuated by one-liners aimed at recapturing or retaining social standing. Hemmings and his like, if they were lucky enough to have tickets, would be in a pub somewhere in Twickenham, on a different socio-economic planet to us. And if they didn't have tickets, they'd be getting stuck into fry-ups and pints of Friary Meux at the club before watching the game on the TV mounted on the wall.

I mention the first time I came, the time with James, because it is the only time I can remember enjoying the experience in an unalloyed way. There is a photo of Uncle Kenneth talking to James and me, both of us with England scarves wrapped tightly around our necks to keep out the cold. All three faces are deadly serious. We're talking about players and tactics.

I've watched many fabulous matches at Twickenham since, but always after an obligatory bathe in the West Stand car park shark pool. The feeling begins the moment I turn into the car park, which is reserved for debenture ticket holders. That feeling of not belonging rises up through my stomach, slowing my walk to crawl. I buy a programme to delay the moment of arrival and give me something to read when I'm there if it all gets too much. Better to see them first than be spotted and called over, several faces turning at once. There's Dad's Range Rover, Uncle Peter's hat with the furry ear flaps. Go over to Dad. Stiff greeting. Talk to whomever Dad is with for a minute or two. Told to go and say hello to Mummy, continental kisses all round.

'James! How are you?' It's Dr Fisher. 'Tell me, what are you doing now?' Ruffles my hair (whether I'm 10, 20 or 30). 'Still doing a bit of the old James Joyce?' That must be a reference to my writing.

'Hello, Dr Fisher,' I say. 'That's me! No full stops and commas!' And I'm off, a performing seal for two hours, powered by Whiskey Mac and pork pies.

If I had to distil into one moment what it meant to grow

up adopted, it would be that. Almost part of the Twickers crowd, almost a braying public schoolboy, almost a Mulholland. Almost, but not quite. And not Hemmings either. It was too late for me to be reinvented as the person I might have been: the unadopted child of my birth mother, grown up. I was somewhere in the ether between the biological son of Alison that I could have been, and the biological son of the Mulhollands that I should be.

Phil Blakeway was my hero; I should say my other hero, along with Phil of the Human League. A Gloucester, England and Lions prop, his Popeye biceps kept his rolled up sleeves permanently wedged into his armpits. I never saw his back bend. I never saw him run with the ball either, but no matter. The man was a scrummaging machine. No opposite number came away from 90 minutes with Phil Blakeway complaining about raw shoulders; they were glad they had shoulders at all! I had a picture of him on my desk, next to the regulatory babes in bikinis torn from Sunday supplements.

After our home matches most of the Cranford 1st XV would go to the King's Arms, an old hotel in the centre of town, where parents of players would stand pints for their sons and friends. The manager, a friendly and astute man in equal measure, turned a watchful/blind eye to the underage drinking that took place in his establishment. One could imagine a parent knowing his employer and having him replaced if he didn't play ball, so maybe he didn't have a lot of choice. It was fun though. With cuts above our eyes and lungs still tingling, we got tanked up and enjoyed being young and fit, our futures ahead of us.

At the end of the season, Dad bought the whole team, together with the coach and his wife, a slap-up dinner in the King's Arms' function room. Boys came up to me throughout the evening, not sure whether to thank me or my dad, who was not there. I made a cheeky toast, thanking the coach's wife for getting me into the team.

Everyone laughed. Everyone had a good time. I had a good time. It was a wonderful end to the season. But I did feel awkward. My dad had come to virtually every match I'd played in and, if that wasn't proof enough of his love, dedication, even – dare I say it – admiration for me, he threw a big party at the end in the team's honour. It was almost like he was saying thank you to us! And a part of me saw this and appreciated it, while another part, the runt trussed up like Little Lord Fauntleroy, felt as if Dad were thanking the rest of the team for accepting me. When you believe you're special and odd, every action by others is seen through a lens of suspicion.

6

Fear

I had managed to secure a job at a newspaper covering the Middlesex area, starting as soon as I completed the journalism course at Cornwall College.

My first story as a salaried reporter concerned a pony that had been "kidnapped" from a field at night. Over the next few months I had plenty of opportunity to sharpen my tabloid writing style, covering a council's decision to ban bunting at an annual fair, which the event organiser slammed as 'bureaucracy gone mad'; the repeated targeting of a cricket pavilion by vandals; and the story of a terrified mother and daughter who huddled together all night without sleeping after their bungalow was ransacked. My big scoop came when a widow of 75 suffering from arthritis contacted me, claiming she had been struck off her doctor's books, at just two weeks' notice, because he disliked visiting her smoky home. When the story attracted the attention of the nationals, and the lady even got to be on the *Jimmy Young Show*, I wrote a follow-up article on the "media circus" that my report of the previous week had precipitated.

I still hadn't passed my 100 words per minute

shorthand test, however, so I was not yet a qualified journalist. This meant having to practise dictation from tapes for twenty minutes every morning before going to work. I was living in a damp house in which every available room was rented out. The only communal area was the kitchen. Oh, and the water came out of the shower in a lukewarm drizzle. But the crappy accommodation – arranged during a flying visit from Cornwall – wasn't the worst of it. There was crackling tension between another tenant and me. The 22-year-old buck, a trainee solicitor, had done something or other to annoy me and I'd told him, very calmly, that I didn't respect him as a person. He never forgave me (as if we were two Mafiosi), which suited me fine, because I WAS TOO FUCKING GOOD FOR THIS PLACE. I resented having to do extra work to get a stupid certificate. I resented having to slum it in a shit-hole a mile-and-a-half from the nearest station. And I resented having no social life and having to take a bottle of wine home and drink alone in a room with a bald electric-blue carpet and chipboard fittings. I was a Mulholland, *they* were lucky to have *me*.

Looking back I can see it didn't have to be like that. On a trip to the south-east for my interview at the newspaper, I'd met a French girl, Francine, in a pub in London and we'd started talking. I told her the amazing story of how I met Alison and she seemed absorbed. She had long black curly hair and a pout. I was beginning to see some payback from being adopted.

When I was next in London Francine cooked me a meal in her flat in Finsbury Park. There she told me her dream was to make lots of money and start her own restaurant in Paris. She spoke gushingly about her best friend, a gay black guy who lived in a funky Paris loft and who she loved more than anyone else in the world. More than me? I remember thinking.

She kissed me with soft pecks, like a small bird with a

velvet glove over its beak, which I found endearing despite preferring the sloppier variety. In bed she kept her white games socks on, which I found kinky. She was exotic, interesting, sensitive and she seemed to like me. But sitting up in her bed afterwards, my face blank and my back rigid, I remember thinking, 'She's not my type: too materialistic. Imagine having a dream to make lots of money!' When we parted the next morning, no plans were made for another meeting.

Even so, the damage was far from irreparable. Why then, as I sat on my bed surrounded by rotting plaster and furnishings that looked as if they'd been salvaged from a skip, did I not think to give her a call? Don't give me any rubbish about too materialistic or not quite connecting in bed. I chose a bottle of sour Chianti and the drone of a talk radio programme over being with a lively, attractive, rather mysterious French girl. I must have been out of my mind. Partly I was holding onto a grudge against her for loving the gay guy 'more than anyone else in the world'. I felt that after one meeting with me she should already have been thinking, 'But that could all change . . .'

Deep down, however, I believe that the reason I backed off from Francine was I was too ashamed about not having a life. I didn't believe in myself as a person. The parts of me seemed just that – parts. There was no whole, only a reporter who wasn't sure he wanted to be a reporter, a room in a house I didn't want to be living in, friends I rang on rotation on Saturday morning to see if they wanted to meet up that night and then held a resentment towards if they didn't offer to include me in their arrangements. My parents were a "problem" to be negotiated, my sister I hardly ever spoke to. Who was I? Who would Francine be getting to know? It was a question best avoided.

* * *

After I had been at the newspaper for a few months, the

girlfriend I'd had at university, Mary, rang to say she was over from America for a few weeks and wondered if I'd like to meet for a drink. She was staying with her best friend from St Andrews, who, she said, had a 'gorgeous' house in Wandsworth, 'dream job' in advertising, husband and two kids.

'Someone's moved on,' I said, picturing us all eight years earlier in baggy clothes slouched in front of the TV. Mary agreed, her voice so devoid of jealousy it made you wonder.

Mary and I had been in the same broad circle since our first week at St Andrews but I'd fallen for her boyish looks and manner towards the end of our second year. The first time that she asked me round for dinner, I was three-quarters of an hour late without thought of an explanation. Mary looked a bit put out but maybe also relieved that I'd come at all. It was only when she produced a homemade bake from the oven and lowered it onto the small table in the steamy, cluttered kitchen that I realised why I was here and not in the pub with Charles and Simon. I remember watching her hang the oven gloves back on their hook, pour away the water from the cabbage and drop a knob of butter into the pan, and realising I was entering a new world of softness. I was both thrilled and anxious at the prospect.

The most fun we had was taking the £500 we had each been given by the university to do some Art History research, and driving non-stop from Scotland to Italy during the summer holidays of our third year. Staying in cheap hostels, we visited walled towns on hills whose names were so familiar to us, discovering little-known churches where there might be some dusty painting by a B-list Renaissance artist tucked away in a dank, forgotten chapel. We'd wait until our eyes acclimatised and try to find the influence of Piero or Titian. I have a photo of us in a dark apse with our Italian suede backpacks beside us, a shaft of light hitting us from a high window like a

Rembrandt. Later we would get sloshed on a couple of carafes and giggle and grope our way back to our room.

We never formally split up. Soon after graduation we stayed at my parents' summer house on the coast for a few days before Mary flew home to America. I had vague plans of teaching TEFL in Spain and Mary, who had an Irish as well as US passport and could therefore live indefinitely in Europe, seemed to be putting her own plans on hold until she knew where we stood. I don't remember discussing our future together in any clear way. Possibly Mary wanted to avoid hearing, and I wanted to avoid giving, a straight no. On her last night we put on the *Big Easy* soundtrack after dinner and when it came to Aaron Neville's heart-wrenching falsetto number we slow-danced together in the drawing room, tears rolling down our cheeks. It was almost as if a force inside me greater than love was saying, 'You need to find out who you are first.'

On one surreal day a few years later I helped Mary move from her Manhattan flat-share into her boyfriend's apartment in Brooklyn Heights. But that relationship had ended too, and here we were alone again in someone else's living room, both adults (thirty years old to be exact) and *sans* significant other.

Mary pulled a bottle of wine from her friend's well-stocked rack and we started reminiscing about that trip to Italy. We agreed we should go on another sometime.

How about next week, before she returned to America? I suggested.

I took a week's holiday from the newspaper and we thought it would be fun to drive to Normandy. I was curious to see if she would recognise the car; it was the same one we'd gone to Italy in as undergraduate lovers, only with a few more scrapes.

We stayed in separate rooms in mid-range hotels, visiting the cities with the great Gothic cathedrals: Chartres, Amiens and lastly Rouen. We bought a camembert from a farmer that was so perfect we had flashbacks for days afterwards. We detoured north to see for ourselves the legendary hole in the cliff at Etretat, much-painted by the Impressionists. Deciding to finish our trip in Paris, we found a hotel in St Germain, where Mary had stayed on a previous visit with her mother, and walked to the Marais for dinner . . . via a drink at Les Deux Magots to pay homage to Hemingway, a stroll over the Pont Neuf to see where the wild vagrants of *Les Amants du Pont Neuf* had lived, and a 'butchers', as our Early Renaissance tutor would have said, at the façade of Notre Dame, which we declared the least impressive of the Gothic cathedrals architecturally, but the most impressive in location. We'd always done that, treated past or fictional characters as if they were alive today, and we might come across them – or an empty cigarette packet left by them – at any moment.

After dinner in a cosy, bustling restaurant, we wandered back to the hotel, among twinkly street lights and men with autumn-colour scarves thrown around their necks, arm-in-arm with women in chic macs. By the time we reached the hotel the rest of the night's activity was a foregone conclusion. But the next morning the view wasn't so rosy. I needed to go forwards, not backwards, I told myself. I convinced myself that kissing her had been disturbing, returning me to 21 years old, and I would have to put an end to this doomed venture before it gained momentum.

Mary was upset, accusing me of being selfish and unbelievably insensitive. I agreed. She said, 'You have issues, James.'

'I know,' I replied.

She told me to stop agreeing with her as it was just a way to avoid admitting what I'd done.

I confirmed I would stop, thinking, the sooner we get back to Newhaven the better. 'I'm useless,' I said, meaning it. 'I'm crap.' I genuinely believed I was saving her from a worse fate by calling an end to it now. I didn't say, *I'm ashamed of myself and couldn't bear the focus on me that getting back with you would bring.* But I was beginning to sense that may be the truth of it.

Back in Blighty, I wrote a story for the paper about a parish council planning to give priority to the local boys' football club over the out-of-town rugby club, once the running of the facility had been handed over from the borough. I included a quotation by the Chairman of the parish council, whom I'd interviewed after a council meeting, in which he said that he'd told the rugby club 'its current use of the ground is against our wishes'.

Back came a letter to the Editor, complaining about the accuracy of my report. The Chairman had two main points:

> 1. *The parish is only **in discussion** [his emphasis] with the borough regarding the possible taking over of some of the duties and maintenance of the recreational ground.*
>
> 2. *The parish council's policy is that the recreational ground should be used by the whole community and does not preclude the rugby club from using the pitches.*

He finished with a flourish, stating that if I had been concerned about the accuracy of my remarks, it might have been beneficial for me to look at the minutes of the parish council meetings.

The editor had handed me the letter in his office. Once I finished reading it, he gave me a schoolmaster's look that said, I know you're guilty but propriety dictates I must give you a chance to defend yourself, and told me to fetch my shorthand notes. At my desk I found the place in my notepad but couldn't find the wretched quotation. Thinking back, I remembered I hadn't produced my notebook in front of the red-faced Chairman of the parish council, who I suspected had been boozing prior to the meeting, because I'd felt he was on a roll and it might inhibit him. Perhaps he'd remembered that when the paper came out and reckoned he could therefore challenge me on the accuracy of my reporting. I went back to the Editor with a mixture of anger at not being believed, and fear that I'd be reprimanded and have my reporting freedom curtailed for compromising the paper.

'Why should I believe you over a respected member of the community?' he asked, as I perched on the edge of a chair.

So I'm not respected, is that it? I felt a self-righteous rage bubble up, while at the same time a clever voice inside me retorted, *If you resign you won't have to put up with this shit any more. You've got enough money to get by. Concentrate on your writing rather than wasting your talent on this faceless suit, whose height of ambition is to be the editor of a local rag.* In a steady voice I stated, 'I stand by everything I wrote in the article.'

It seems to me now that the key mistake I'd made was to listen to the rugby club's case and make up my mind before I heard the parish's side. Everyone tweaked quotations to fit word counts and as long as the message was the same, no one minded. My crime was to write an unbalanced report.

He seemed to be looking in the direction of my notepad, which I had allowed to drop out of his line of vision.

'You either believe me or him,' I said. 'And if you believe him, my position at this paper is no longer tenable.' When I think about that line now I instinctively recall what I said to Trevor Burman, the Headmaster at Barton, when he asked me if I'd written the note about stopping taking other boys' underwear. To Burman I'd said, 'I may be able to help you if you tell me what's prescribed on the note.' On both occasions I sound like a helpful observer, using words like tenable and prescribed in an attempt to give the impression of being an intelligent person whose help they would do well to utilise in their current predicament. It is as if the 13-year-old, buoyed by his success in Burman's study, had taken over control when it started getting sticky in the Editor's office. I'll handle this, he said, and the 30-year-old gratefully stepped aside.

I could see him weighing up what I'd said, thinking, *Is this novice trying to bluff me or does he think he's John Pilger?* Eventually he said, 'Frankly, I've known Pete for nigh on twenty years. If he says he didn't say something, I believe him.'

I stood up and said in that case I was resigning. It got a shocked reaction, which kept me going until I reached the news room and had to pack up my things, wondering if everyone somehow knew what had happened. I told the chief sub-editor, a Welshman with tattoos on his arms and a fag permanently in his mouth, that I'd 'resigned over a difference of opinion' with the Editor and he shook my outstretched hand, while probably thinking, *What an idiot to walk out over something like that. That's toffs for you!*

* * *

My immediate solution to being unemployed was to busy myself doing DIY on a house I'd bought in Twickenham. In the back of my mind was the idea I might introduce Dad and Mummy to Alison and Davy by putting on a lunch at my new place. Somehow I didn't get round to it, however. Instead, once I'd had enough of bashing through plasterboard and putting up shelves, I bought a ticket to Hawaii with a view to trying my luck with my other ex-girlfriend, Rita.

I'd met Rita in Norwich while I was on the Creative Writing course, working on my second novel (a few years before the journalism course) and for a year we'd led the hippie lifestyle, cooking lentils and baking bread, strolling through Norfolk countryside and collapsing in pubs with hot faces and pints of real ale. Rita, like Mary, was

American but whereas Mary called Connecticut and New York home, Rita came from Santa Fe, New Mexico, and her outlook was correspondingly more laid back.

About the only thing she had wanted from me other than companionship was a baby. I told her I wasn't ready for children (I couldn't even *imagine* myself as a father), while making it seem as if the situation could change. If she'd asked me if I wanted to join her on a murder spree, I'd have said not right now but maybe in the future. I didn't feel able to close or open the door on anything. And – in a remake of my ending with Mary – Rita and I agreed to live together in America; she flew out first to spend Christmas with her family and I never went out to join her.

The current setup in Hawaii, as I understood it, was that Rita had gone over there to be with her boyfriend, the one after me, and had secured a post as a tutor at the university there. Since then, her boyfriend had got cold feet and returned to New Mexico, leaving Rita with the rental rights on the ground floor of a duplex in Honolulu and a beaten-up soft-top Beetle, for which she'd paid him a hefty $1,000. I arrived on the scene with the first drafts of three short stories, hoping to rekindle something with Rita and write a few more stories to make enough for a collection.

When you arrive in Hawaii the first thing you notice is the intense smell of flowers, and this remains undiminished as you travel into the slow-ticking heart of Honolulu. Rita was at work when I arrived but, as arranged, she'd left a key under a pot. I let myself in, put on the kettle and made some spicy-smelling Hawaiian coffee. I remember being intrigued by a picture of a lion on the packet. Why didn't they have someone dancing in a grass skirt or surfing a tube? The flat was more or less open-plan – a large studio – with partitions built for a bedroom and bathroom. I dropped a Leo Kottke CD into the tray, sat on the sofa and waited for her to come back, listening to finger-picked guitar melodies that seemed to go off on their own before eventually returning home.

Rita had a white father and Hispanic mother, but her features also owed something to her American Indian maternal grandfather. She had an exotic wide face tapering to a narrow chin, oval eyes and long straight hair parted in the middle. It didn't take us long to hop back into bed, and to resume our game of emotional chess.

The first few weeks we played for position. She showed me around the island and talked about her students; I found a secluded desk in the city library at which to work on the stories. Our credentials established, she then asked me if I was planning on staying (white queen emerges from behind a line of pawns).

'I'm not sure,' I say (black pawn blocks white queen's approach).

'Typical male, afraid to commit,' she says (white bishop takes up a position beside his queen).

A few days later we're sitting on a beach, staring at the Pacific. 'I'll stay,' I say (black knight trots into view: check). *Why rush back to England?* I'm thinking. *I'll ring an estate agent and get them to rent my house on a short-term lease. What've I got to lose?*

'OK,' says Rita, looking thoughtful (white king moves out of the line of fire).

'For six months?' I suggest. 'See how we get on.'

Next day I'm cross-legged on the sofa sipping a Hawaiian coffee while she gets ready to leave for college. 'Why can't you clear away anything, I'm not your slave,' she snaps (white knight charges into the fray). She looks like she'd like to swipe the cafetière and plate with crumbs on it I've left on the kitchen surface onto the floor (chessboard in danger of being upended).

I sit there, weightless. She sounds like my mother, and I feel like her teenage son.

When I return from the library that evening, Rita is waiting for me. 'I'm not sure I want you to stay,' she says

157

(white queen puts black in check).

'I thought you were the one who wanted me to stay,' I say (black queen moves into sacrificial position to delay the inevitable execution of the king). I'm put out, how could she not want me? But also secretly relieved. 'I thought I was the one who couldn't commit,' I say. Careful, I'm thinking, you don't want to push her into reconsidering.

(When I phoned her a few years later, having got her UK number from her mother, she told me she'd married – I swear this is true – a boy who was not only an Old Cranfordian but in my year at St B! He'd been doing the same course as her at Norwich. And she was expecting a baby. 'It's so simple with Gary,' she told me, 'with you everything was always complicated.' I felt panicky. Maybe Gary had seen glaringly obvious qualities in Rita I'd missed? Worse, maybe Rita saw qualities in Gary she hadn't seen in me? I tried to console myself with the thought that at least I'd got there first. It was the last time we spoke.)

* * *

Back in Twickenham, the prospect of trying to find a job or a girlfriend was like having to choose whether to climb K2 from the Pakistani or Chinese side. In comparison with these challenges, bringing the Adamses and Mulhollands together under one roof – my roof – seemed like a more manageable adventure.

I half-heartedly phoned around for a hotel but could tell Alison really wanted to stay with me. I was aware this might seem like more recognition than she deserved but in the end, I told myself, it was my home. There was a limit to how much you could tiptoe around people's feelings before you ended up satisfying no one. Secretly, however, I knew I wanted Alison and Davy to stay with me in order to show my parents who was boss. So Alison and Davy slept in the spare room and the next morning, while she helped me prepare the meal, Davy puffed on his pipe and read the paper.

Mendelssohn's violin concerto twisted mournfully on the turntable as I introduced my parents to Alison and Davy. Immediately, amazingly, while I stood holding the pudding – which I'd asked Mummy to make in order to counter the recognition I'd given Alison in having her stay with me – the two mums hugged like long-lost relatives, cried, and didn't stop talking for the rest of the day.

It was warm and sunny, and Alison and I had carried the dining table into the garden. When I wasn't ferrying dishes to and from the kitchen, I sat floating in a haze of far-off traffic sounds, neighbours' voices and red wine, pretending to take it all in my stride. Mummy's accent, which could become cut-glass when she had something to prove, was reassuringly natural. Alison wasn't laughing outrageously. And Dad and Davy, a rugby second row and prop respectively, were discussing rugby in all its minutiae with only marginally less passion than the women discussed – I have no idea what they discussed.

If anything, the day seemed to be going off suspiciously, even disappointingly smoothly. I did wonder if out of courtesy to me the mums might not have got on quite so well. There seemed to be not a trace of bitterness or rivalry between them. It was as if all my anxiety and shame about being adopted was exactly that, my anxiety and shame. See how the grown-ups put things in perspective and get along, I told myself sarcastically. I was tempted to feel as if the only obstacle to the party being a roaring success was my presence; at least that way I had a decent grievance to nurture. (What I didn't do was put myself in their shoes. Despite the outpouring of emotion, the two women were clearly on best behaviour, which, however you looked at it, was a compliment to me.)

I'm not sure how well I managed the leaving. Alison and Davy were staying a second night so the three of us waved my parents off from the white picket fence in front of my house. The symbolism must have been hard for my parents.

Nevertheless, from that day on I have always felt that Mummy and Alison had more in common than I had with Alison. And while it was galling to see Mummy take over my find, it was also a relief to share the responsibility for fielding Alison's emotions. The more hand-holding and weeping they did together, the less I had to do.

*   *   *

I got a job as a barman at Blake's Brasserie in Richmond. The high concept was that it would get me out of the house, meeting new people when I wasn't sitting in front of a computer writing stories. Alison, endearingly, seemed to take the job at face value, congratulating me on the appointment. I'm not sure what my parents thought. Probably, more realistically, they saw it as better than nothing. Of course there's nothing wrong with being a barman, unless you're doing it to punish people.

To get to work I cycled along the footpath beside the Thames. In the autumn and winter it was often misty and the trees and bushes beside the path had a potent smell that made you feel part of the earth. Occasionally you passed a moored barge linked to the land by a plank. You could tell if the owner of one in particular was aboard by whether his bicycle was chained to the tree. It had to be a man, only males choose to live below the surface of the earth, alone.

The area behind the bar, which was only really big enough for one person, was my little world at Blake's. As long as I kept the fridges stocked with cold beer and the bowl of lemon wedges full, there was practically nothing that could go wrong. I prepared drinks for the waiters, sometimes carrying them to a table when I had the time to help out, but I didn't take orders from punters and therefore handled no cash. The only thing that made one day different from another was how fast I had to work, but the routine was always the same. I looked forward to the occasional table that wanted six different cocktails; it made for a change.

I'd been a waiter a few years back and it had been far more demanding. But the reason I was glad not to be waiting tables at Blake's was I'd found it too easy in the past to slip into being a performing seal as I went around trying to judge each table's mood and give them the kind of waiter they wanted, and would tip. The self-containment of bar work suited me better. Anyway, tips were pooled at Blake's – though not quite evenly.

I shared the bar rota with Karl, a German who had started at Blake's a few months before me. We left notes to each other, mostly about stock levels, sometimes continuing a running joke. There was a patch when we quoted lines from a song and the other had to write down what came next. We liked some of the same music, Radiohead, REM, The Doors, which made the game easier. Karl was a musician and composer and I started going round to his house once a week for acoustic guitar lessons. His American wife had been a Moonie before marrying him and, it transpired, she too had been adopted. When I met her I was amazed at how perky she was, though I'm not sure if my amazement was caused by knowing she was adopted, an ex-Moonie, or married to watchful, guarded Karl. But the strangest moment I had with him was during a guitar lesson, when I asked him about growing up in Germany and he told me he wasn't German.

'But everyone at Blake's thinks you are!' I said. 'The first thing Jules told me was I would be sharing the bar rota with a German.' That didn't come out quite right, or rather it came out exactly as Jules had said it. Jules, the deputy manager, found Karl's reserved nature unnerving and seemed to have conveniently put it down to his being German. A Tunisian, Jules regularly made jokes about 'the Nazi table' if a punter had cropped or flaxen hair, which helped to contextualise further his "mistake" about Karl's nationality.

Karl smiled in a self-contained way, his fingers finding chords but not actually strumming them.

'You must be a bit German,' I went on. 'I mean, you sound – you've got a bit of a Teutonic accent, wouldn't you say?'

'My father was part German,' he said. 'I told Jules that once and . . .' he smiled to himself again.

I looked at him as neutrally as possible. That *Fawlty Towers* episode was correct: it was near-impossible for an Englishman not to think of the Second World War when meeting a German for the first time.

'I've spent my whole life in England. No, I lie, I went to Boulogne on a school trip.'

As I listened to him speak I realised there was nothing Germanic about his accent at all. He was simply reserved. It affected me quite deeply. I couldn't understand why he wouldn't put the matter straight, how he could be happy for everyone at his place of work to think he was something he wasn't. I thought of all the times I'd chosen a simpler word to explain something, or slowed down my speech when speaking to him. It must have seemed like I thought he was simple. Karl appeared to be watching me with quiet amusement, so I flung myself into one of the Simon and Garfunkel songs I'd been practising.

Jules arranged it so that his girlfriend, a large-boned beautiful woman called Florence, and he were always on the same shift. I got to know Florence quite well. She'd left school after her GCSEs and only really wanted to be a mother. What she was doing with Jules, I didn't know. She lacked confidence and maybe he'd scooped her up and now she couldn't imagine life without him.

Once, I was talking to Florence during the lull at the end of the lunch shift and Jules came over, wearing his usual smirk and chewing gum. She asked him if she could have a piece and he took the white ball from his mouth and offered it to her. 'I don't want that!' she said.

Jules replied, 'You've had my cock in your mouth, what's wrong with a bit of gum?'

I betrayed Florence with the faintest laugh born of shock and a desire not to antagonise my deputy manager. Jules, I suppose, was making it clear I'd been talking to Florence on loan from him. To my eyes, she appeared hurt, but she could have been feeling a whole lot of other things I wouldn't have a clue about. She might have felt she deserved it.

Another person Jules put down was a sad guy about my age called Mick, who came to Blake's most days during the quiet time after lunch for a hot chocolate. Jules often gave it to him on the house, and then didn't stop reminding him that this wasn't a soup kitchen. On the days Mick didn't come, Jules let it slip that he missed Mick by continually referring to his absence, even if it was to make comments like, 'He probably choked on a Prozac tablet. Why doesn't he give them to me, I'd enjoy taking them!'

One night Mick came by near closing time for a change. Jules wasn't on duty, and we got talking about music. He said he'd been to one of the last concerts by Karen Carpenter before she became seriously ill from 'complications resulting from an eating disorder'. He sounded like he was reading from a prepared statement. Mick asked me if I wanted to watch a video of the Carpenters in concert back at his place. I wondered if he had something funny in mind, but one look at his puppy eyes told me he simply wanted company.

He had a nice flat, subsidised by Richmond Council on account of his depression, but there were no personal touches that I could see, not even a poster on the wall or empty beer bottle from the night before. He made me a cup of tea and we watched Karen Carpenter sing her mournful songs about lost love and alienation. Why doesn't he say anything? I thought. Why doesn't he run into Blake's right now and shout at Jules, 'I'm not gonna put up with your shit any more! Either treat me like a human being or don't talk to me at all.'

But he wouldn't, couldn't. Maybe it was the medication, but he'd rather sit here with some guy he hardly knew, getting even more depressed listening to the Carpenters. Why didn't Florence say anything, why didn't Karl say anything? Why didn't I say anything? I was starting to feel paranoid. How many people in Richmond at this moment had convinced themselves they'd rather stay silent than risk the consequences? I thought of the Beatles lines, *All the lonely people / where do they all come from*? If we could see the insides of people we'd see a very different story.

I waited until the end of 'Goodbye to Love' and told Mick I'd see myself to the door.

* * *

'Read this,' Will, my friend from Cranford, said, handing me a book with a long title and minimal graphics on the cover. 'It's about us.' Will explained that the author was his therapist. Once he'd left, I made some herbal tea to suit the New Age subject, curled up on the sofa like an innocent kitten – telling myself it would be interesting to see inside Will's mind – and started reading.

It was all about a psychological disturbance called *co-dependency*. This term appeared to have originally been used to describe the unconscious collusive behaviour of an alcoholic's partner. For example, a wife might secretly wish her husband to continue drinking so that she could continue being a victim, receiving sympathy from friends and feeling like a saint. However, the term's usage had since been broadened to refer to anyone whose self-worth was dependent on the way others saw them. The 'tragedy of co-dependency' was that the sufferer existed in a manufactured personality designed to please others and make an impression. The co-dependent often reported feeling 'empty inside' or 'like a total fake'.

I couldn't stop gasping, dropping the book and calling into the air things like, 'That's me . . . Spot on . . . *The agony.*' The only part I wasn't certain about was pleasing others, in terms of my parents. Hadn't I more often been trying to displease them, particularly since leaving university? A chapter on, the answer was supplied: emotions were essentially conservative; they stuck with what they knew. If you grew up believing that what was expected of you was to be a chump, whenever you behaved like one, you felt valued. It became your role, whether it be in the family unit, classroom or playground. In this way negative attention became its own reward. But the cost for the chump was that he remained stuck in his childhood programming; he hadn't 'become his own person'.

So I was special and odd, a chump, because the childish part of me still thought it was what my parents expected! What they wanted even, if they were co-dependent too and relied on my behaving in a certain way for their own self-worth. Presumably everyone was a bit co-dependent. I can remember feeling paradoxically excited at the discovery of this psychological condition called co-dependency, which seemed to fit me so well.

It also implied that being co-dependent wasn't my fault. Not all my fault, anyway.

Unbeknownst to me, I was now entering a perilous state of mind which, if left unchecked, could suck you into a lifetime of playing the victim. 'Look at what was done to me,' was dangerous talk unless accompanied by, 'and look at what I have done to make it ten times worse.' Re-reading the book now, I can see that the author makes it clear it's not what happens to you but how you react to it that decides how you feel about something. But that wasn't the message I came away with on that first reading. I thought I'd found a psychological theory to support something I'd always believed: my parents were to blame for how I felt. All I had to do now, the last chapter said, was... get a therapist. The address of the hospital where the author practised was written on the back cover.

Understandably Will didn't fancy sharing his therapist with me. Instead he gave me the number of Dr Fellows, a GP who operated as a kind of therapy middleman, assessing your condition before recommending the best course of action. It was how Will had found his guy.

I wondered how many other Old Cranfordians had been through Fellows's door. It is curious that neither the Barton House nor Cranford School websites make any mention of the additional expense of five years' therapy that should be put aside for later on in life.

A receptionist showed me to the wood-panelled waiting room of Fellows's Knightsbridge practice. After she'd left me alone, I approached the mahogany dining table in the centre of the room, on which a tray with bottles of still and sparkling mineral water and glasses had been placed. Either side of the refreshment was a fan of magazines, from *Hello* to *New Scientist*. Above the fireplace hung an oil painting of a hunting scene, and the thought came to me that I could put it under my coat and walk out. I rejected the magazines and sat down on one of the overstuffed pastel sofas that lined the room. I hadn't even asked how much the appointment would cost. Probably £50, maybe £100. I peered inside my jacket to make sure my cheque book and wallet were ready and waiting. *What are you getting yourself into? This setup is out of your league, the kind of place you find in Harley Street.* Eventually the receptionist returned and led me to Dr Fellows's consultancy room.

It didn't take long for me to start sobbing uncontrollably. Fellows pushed a box of Kleenex across his desk. He kept his thick wiry hair brushed straight back, lending it what I imagined was an unintentional bouffant, but otherwise he looked every bit the sober businessman:

pin-stripe suit, manicured nails and a silver fountain pen with gold trim, the last poised to write notes about my condition. Once I'd got myself together again, he said, 'What's your poison?'

I looked at him blankly.

The most mobile part of Fellows's otherwise composed face were his thick wiry eyebrows, which seemed to respond to subtle shifts in mood that even you, their instigator, might otherwise have missed. This time they rose and contracted simultaneously, seeming to indicate a state between amusement and empathy. 'How do you cope? What gets you through the night?'

I saw where he was going, but decided to delay admitting this. I found his eyebrows oddly comforting and wanted to sit listening to him and watching them for a few seconds longer.

'Alcohol, pot, cocaine, heroin,' he listed, his eyebrows at their most placid and accepting, 'promiscuity, binge-eating, twenty cups of coffee a day?'

'Probably alcohol out of that lot,' I said. It was on the edge of my tongue to say, 'I should be so lucky to have promiscuity as a problem!' but thankfully I kept quiet. I must be getting better already, I thought.

I told Fellows I had two or three whiskeys every night and felt it helped me fall asleep. He recommended I attend Alcoholics Anonymous. 'It's a fine organisation, and if it's not for you, you've lost nothing,' he said in a low, reassuring voice. He gave me a choice of two therapists, a Polish lady who he said was very understanding and an American lady who he said was 'tough'. I, of course, chose the American lady because what I needed was to be picked up by the scruff of the neck and dragged into adulthood, right? No gooey 'love' for my 'pain', I needed a headmistress from hell. (Only years later did I find out that Fellows specialised in addiction. According to my source, he was so versed in an alcoholic's denial that he automatically doubled the number of drinks you admitted to having and made each a large one, which certainly explained his concern about my alcohol consumption. When I asked Will how he'd escaped being sent to AA, he said he'd told the good doctor he rarely drank at all during the week – the liar!)

I got what I asked for in Beth Madison. She listened to my adoption/spoilt little rich boy story, made some perfunctory sympathetic noises and asked me how much I really drank ('Two to three whiskeys or the equivalent on weekdays, four to five on weekends'). She gave me the first of many heavy-lidded looks and asked me if that included the drinks I helped myself to behind the bar at Blake's when no one was watching. How did she know that? I chuckled nervously, then said, 'Yes'. Next she wanted to know how often I 'used' pornographic images ('Sometimes') and objectified women's bodies ('Quite a bit'). This got not only a heavy-lidded look but a clipped 'Yeah' that seemed more for herself than me.

I gave her an easy-going smile, hoping to place my answers in the context of what a nice guy I was. Surely looking at porn occasionally didn't make me – and most other males in Britain, I suspected – into a sex fiend? But maybe it did. Maybe I simply had a particularly bad case of being male? My easy-going smile had probably looked like a Hannibal Lecter leer from her side of the desk.

Beth turned to a white board on the wall behind her and drew an "onion" diagram, writing the word Co-dependency at the centre and then adding various addictions in layers around the outside. Each addiction – sex, alcohol, food, work, even adrenalin – was an attempt to anaesthetise the "wounded child" within, she explained. Only when an addict stopped "using" could they begin to treat the underlying condition of low self-esteem. She strongly advised me to attend not only AA but also Sex Addicts Anonymous and possibly also Coda (Codependents Anonymous). Overnight I had a full diary. What did I have to lose? Anyway Beth was too intimidating to disobey openly.

We also agreed that bar work was probably not the best employment for a recovering alcoholic, as I was learning to consider myself. I rang Blake's from a phone box outside Beth's office and Jules picked up. 'I can't work at Blake's any more,' I blurted out. 'I think I might be an alcoholic.' The more you said the word, the easier it became. Jules tried to get me to talk with the general manager before making a final decision, but I was adamant, and with a philosophical sigh he wished me luck. I remember thinking, I bet you're one too. Later I would learn to interpret this as the envious response of a recovering alcoholic to anyone still tucking into the juice without a care.

I can remember sitting in my first AA meeting, staring at the close-cropped grey hair and ghoulishly dented skull of the man in the row in front of me, thinking, I am a flawed human being. It struck me as a desperately sad statement. I wondered if, rather than entering a phase of recovery, I was actually taking the first step towards insanity.

'Welcome to the human race,' Beth said with a grin when I told her about my thoughts in my first meeting.

Just as an alcoholic needs an ever-increasing number of drinks to feel drunk (until his body starts to degenerate and then he needs less and less), so I found myself collecting more and more "Anonymous" titles. The first sex meeting was scary. What if the police were here doing undercover work on a prostitution racket or paedophile ring and decided to take us all down to the station for an identification parade? But during coffee and biscuits after the meeting, which took place in the unheated crypt of a church in Victoria, I discovered that all seven of the attendees were friendly, earnestly trying to deal with their "addiction" to porn, prostitutes or (the SAA aristocracy) serial affairs – and in therapy with either Beth Madison or the Polish lady!

After that there was no holding me back. On Monday evenings I went to SAA in Victoria, on Tuesdays I saw Beth, Wednesdays I went to my local AA meeting in Teddington, Thursdays I had the choice of attending the Hinde Street Al-Anon meeting for Adult Children of Alcoholics (after all, Dad drank as much as, if not more than me!) or taking a day off (later, it became my afternoon to man the AA switchboard). On Fridays I could fit in a 6pm near to wherever I was going out afterwards, and on Saturdays I attended the civilised 10am gathering in W14. But Sunday was the pièce de résistance, the up yours to Beth, when I attended the Twickenham afternoon meeting of Overeaters Anonymous.

'Might that be overdoing it a bit?' Beth suggests.

'Once you eliminate your addictions of choice, it's all too easy to replace them with new compulsive behaviour,' I explain, quoting from the latest co-dependency book I've read. 'I feel there can be a driven quality to my eating. When I'm feeling vulnerable I often eat until I'm absolutely full. I also find myself darting into corner shops to buy Minstrels when I'm not even hungry – just because they are there. I don't drink, I don't masturbate, I apply the three second rule as best I can' (1. Catch yourself objectifying a woman's body; 2. Remove your eyes from the target; 3. Ask yourself how you're feeling, in order to shed light on the uncomfortable emotional state that you've been trying to distract yourself from through objectification) 'so I give myself the entitlement' – not *I feel entitled*, because I aim to take full responsibility for my actions – 'to have chocolate whenever I want. That sounds to me like substituting food for alcohol and sex.'

Hands meekly folded on my lap, I give Beth a look that I hope conveys my genuine dilemma about what I've just said. On the one hand: *If you believe that pile of crap you're more stupid than I thought*. On the other hand: *It may just be true*.

Beth smiles wryly and lets my speech and concomitant look pass by innocuously. She knows what I'm up to. About the least destructive thing an addict can do is become addicted to meetings. She tells me she wonders if I've chosen to go to OA in order to downgrade the importance of my sex and alcohol addiction?

'I get it,' I say. "Like I'm saying 'I'm clearly not really a food addict and yet I attend their meeting, so maybe the same can be said about alcohol and sex? I'm just here for the ride".'

Beth nods encouragingly. *This guy's good*, I hope she's thinking. And at the same time I can see myself completing the full circle of co-dependent behaviour: I'm trying to please the therapist. I want to be a text book co-dependent, in order to fit into Beth's world view and make her feel right.

Apart from the structure the various "Anonymous" meetings gave my life, what I got most out of them was the camaraderie. The back of my diary was full of names and telephone numbers, with *SAA, AA, AlAnon* or *OA* after each. I soon discovered that sharing honestly at meetings and afterwards with people over coffee was fun, and that chattering about nothing with friends felt like hard work. I found out, as Beth had intimated would happen, that I liked being with other flawed humans. There was no feeling or thought I couldn't tell another member of the fellowship, however petty, needy or vindictive. I felt accepted. Even – after three months without a drink or touching the fella in lust – a star.

As to whether I was really an alcoholic, sex addict or even overeater, deep-down I remained undecided. I figured I used to drink only a few glasses more than your average 30-year-old male over a week, but maybe I'd relied on them more. Certainly a night without a drink would have lacked something. Compared to almost every drinking story I'd heard in meetings so far, however, my consumption had been lame. But as my AA sponsor, a generous open-minded man whose home I visited every fortnight to go through the Twelve Steps of Recovery, pointed out to me, 'Better to be unsure and in the programme, than unsure and drinking.'

I can see him smiling through years of experience. 'Only an alcoholic can't bear the thought of not having a drink.' In other words, if you're not an alcoholic, what harm can be done by abstaining from drink for a while and improving your emotional well-being through completing the Twelve Steps?

I had no answer, and anyway, being a good co-dependent, I wanted to please him, Beth and all my new friends too much to back out now. They'd only nod their heads solemnly, wish me luck and think, *See you next week/year/in your coffin.*

With porn it was harder to tell. You couldn't get the average recovering alcoholic to give you a straight answer on that subject, nor did I feel able to ask my friends about it other than in the vaguest way. Sean, also single, admitted to 'a swimwear catalogue or a girly mag once in a while,' with a nonchalant shrug that made it clear he didn't see the point in discussing the matter further. Compared with the danger of Aids that guys with promiscuity issues exposed themselves to, my porn use seemed relatively innocuous. In the end, whichever group I was attending, I never seemed able to say with conviction that critical first step of the programme: 'We admitted we were powerless over alcohol/our addictive sexual behaviour/food and that our lives had become unmanageable.'

Somehow, I'd contrived to find another place where I felt as if I didn't quite belong.

'Has your life become unmanageable?' Beth asked me.

'Yes.' Although the truth was that anything more strenuous than a stroll to a local meeting followed by coffee began to look "unmanageable" after a while.

'Well then, you're halfway there.'

Looking back, I think the main attraction of defining myself as an alcoholic was to show everyone, most of all myself and my parents, what a terrible person I was. I'd always known I was a terrible person and here for the first time was concrete proof of how terrible I was. When the chance to be a sex addict came along, I naturally leapt at that too, though I knew enough not to go around advertising it outside of Twelve-Step meetings (as the various types of "Anonymous" meeting were collectively known as). If alcoholism showed how out of control I was, sex addiction showed how dirty I was deep inside. It took my terribleness one stage further. 'This is what happens,' I wanted the world to know, 'when you give a baby up for adoption.'

I got part-time work as an assistant at Waterstone's bookshop. I'd always liked the calm atmosphere in their stores and the friendly way staff seemed to have with each other. It didn't take long, however, for me to be called into the manager's office and given a last warning for swearing down the phone at another member of staff who I felt had given me attitude.

Needless to say Beth found the incident instructive, explaining to me it was 'typical addict behaviour – in the old days,' she said, 'you would've had a drink or used pornographic images to medicate your anger. Now you don't have those crutches: whoosh, out it comes! Anger is good, rage is bad.' We spent the rest of the session working on ways to stop the volcano erupting.

I did wonder, as I walked back to the tube station, however, if I'd unconsciously exploded in the first place in order to give Beth the chance to show me how co-dependent I was, and therefore how right she was. If she was right, and therefore safe in the world, it followed that I, who was in her care, was also safe.

Next step, Beth informed me after six months of therapy, was to check into The Lodge in Arizona for four weeks of residential treatment. This was where she'd trained and it was the leading addiction clinic in the world. Part of the programme involved Family Week, where members of your family came to the clinic to help work through the unresolved family issues that always underpinned co-dependency. 'I think that part would be particularly helpful in your case,' she said.

'My parents – Arizona – treatment centre?' The idea moved swiftly from preposterous, to hilarious, to appalling.

Beth sat there behind her desk, watching me incuriously. Behind Beth her different colour markers sat patiently on their tray under the whiteboard, waiting to be used to draw an addiction onion for the next depraved male that came through the door. Not for the first time, I thought there was a pinched quality about her. I could imagine her in a Victorian girdle, telling her maid to fasten it tighter. *Tighter, I said!* She was a female Malvolio, an American Puritan of the late twentieth century. The only thing better than indulgence was not indulging. A thought struck me: I wonder if she gets a kick out of all this? First it's meetings, now a treatment centre. But I knew I'd go. I had travelled too far along this path to back out now.

'They might want Alison to come out too.'

'You've got to be joking!' I blurted out. 'I . . . Wh . . . Hmm.' Strangely I felt more protective of Alison than my parents, who I felt could look after themselves. Or maybe I wanted to maintain the illusion with Alison of being in control of my life. Whereas with my parents a part of me relished the idea of rubbing their faces in my failure, even as another part recoiled from any hazy ideas I had of what might actually take place there. The only concrete scenario I could come up with was my parents arriving at the treatment centre in the sizzling Arizona desert, my dad's eyes blanked out by his aviator sunglasses and my mum in white linen, and Dad handing the driver a handsome tip.

I'm watching them from a high window, a look of terror clouding my face.

7
Anger

I was put in Blue Group. It was generally understood that this was where they put the male sex addicts, although I never heard this confirmed by anyone in authority. This didn't seem, at least at the time, as bad as it may sound. For one thing, "sex addict" did not equate with "pervert" within the confines of an American rehab. Also, alcoholics, drug abusers and foodies seemed to have their own groups so we were not being singled out on that count.

Groups met every morning for a couple of hours of counselling. The first time you spoke it was expected you would introduce yourself in the time-honoured way of Alcoholics Anonymous. Our counsellor began, 'Name's Roy, cocaine addict, alcoholic, sex addict, abused growing up on the streets'a De-troit.' He stressed the first syllable of 'Detroit' like some Americans say 'A-rab' or 'I-raq'.

A burly man in his forties, Roy had a close-cropped beard over pockmarked skin, and sat with his right ankle resting on his left knee. The only detail to contradict this manly demeanour was his tasselled loafers, the right one lolling coquettishly off the side of his left knee. I can remember noticing his feet were also on the petite side but he couldn't help that, although he did pull his skin-tight cotton socks high up his calf. Perhaps he had patchy leg hair, or it could have been a Lodge regulation that counsellors cover up areas of their bodies that could conceivably excite patients. *Didn't they know covering up was what made it interesting?* No doubt I was both intrigued and put off by this mix of masculine and feminine because I recognised it in myself.

The Lodge, like other rehabs based on the Twelve Steps, prided itself on employing only recovering addicts. This way patients could be sure their counsellors spoke from experience and understood what they were going through. Roy let it be known he'd been sober – a term that embraced abstinence from addictive sexual behaviour as well as from booze and drugs – for ten years, every day of which he considered a bonus, a gift from his 'Higher Power'.

When one of us started talking about Eric Clapton's song 'Cocaine', Roy silenced him mid-sentence. 'We don't have euphoric recall in here,' he said. 'I hear that song now, I switch it off if I'm in a position to do so. Or I walk out the room. I start to think it's OK to listen, before I know it . . .' he was clearly growing agitated. 'I got a wife and young kid I love. Like that, I could lose everything.'

Silence followed, during which he made no attempt to wipe away the tears clinging to his eyelids. It was not the most comforting of displays considering his audience, but it was real. You could feel the beat of your heart. You sensed a life in the palm of a hand. For those of us sleepwalking through our lives, that had to be a good thing.

Gradually members of Blue Group revealed bits and pieces of our own back-stories, sometimes with the help of Roy, who'd studied what records had been passed The Lodge's way via the police, hospitals and therapists. Marty, a middle-aged company executive who dressed smart-casual, had a quiet confidence about him. A week into my stay, Roy asked him out of the blue, 'Marty, you gonna tell us why you're here?'

Marty mumbled he supposed he'd let his drinking get out of hand.

'I was wondering,' Roy said, 'if you were going to tell us about swinging your partner around the bedroom by her nipples?'

Marty's face said he hadn't planned bringing that up.

Roy informed us that Doyle, a cone-shaped man as bleached and formless as a melting snowman, was one drink away from death. No one in Blue Group except Doyle seemed to doubt it. After a session, Doyle confided in me that he'd been dry for a year until his last relapse, when he'd been feeling low and for some unknown reason had decided to pour himself a Southern Comfort and 7Up in the safety of his home. Next thing he knew he was in casualty. I nodded grimly. Anything I could think of to say seemed too late. He was melting away before my eyes.

Lars, a blond Danish-American buck in his early thirties, told Blue Group with a laconic chuckle that he treated a deal of things about The Lodge with a pinch of salt. Roy reminded him there'd be more than a pinch of earth sprinkled on his coffin if he carried on with that attitude. Jerome, of an aristocratic Memphis family, liked his girlfriend to stand over him while he looked up her skirt, which Roy found 'very dangerous behaviour'. And Frank, a tall thin man, had left his wife, two young daughters and business one day and moved to Denver, without a forwarding address. A nervous breakdown soon followed. It must have had something to do with his father sexually abusing him as a boy, we all agreed. But no one felt able to say more. The thing we all apparently had in common was we were sex addicts. It was bewildering, which didn't necessarily make it wrong.

I did everything that was asked of me. I shared as truthfully as I could, from telling Blue Group about wearing other boys' woollen underwear at prep school, to admitting to a trip to Amsterdam with university friends that, by itself, would have qualified all of us for lifetime membership of every Twelve-Step fellowship in Christendom. Those two confessions neatly book-ended my 'shares': the first showing I was brave enough to expose my most shameful inner self, the second that I accepted I was *one of them* to the extent that I could laugh about the crazy things us addicts got ourselves into. Of course, I had a hidden agenda, the same one I'd had when explaining to Beth back in England why I had needed to attend so many different types of Twelve-Step meetings. I hoped everyone would think that only someone who wasn't a full-blown addict could so freely admit to being one. In this way I could feel as if I were both inside the group and above it.

Once I got the hang of group counselling, it became a matter of pride that I would share with more startling truthfulness than anyone else. I can remember my heart racing as I told Blue Group that I got a sadistic thrill out of hearing the details of other members' troubles.

Making no distinction between honesty and truth, I was simply following the creed that, if it were true, it must be said. I did not see the dishonesty at the heart of such truth-telling, or "sharing" as it was called. As I had done with the Creative Writing group a few years earlier, I was hoping to claim a place for myself within the group as Speaker of the Unspeakable. And the only way to secure such a post was to make a show of being prepared to risk expulsion from the group. In this way I was a pseudo-Brutus, having to persuade the group of my honourable intentions, while blood dripped from my hands. Of course, Brutus had real integrity, whereas I only thought I had it. Fortunately Roy was no Mark Antony and the mob was left impressed by my performance at best, only riled at worst.

* * *

The daily routine at The Lodge consisted of attending

179

group counselling and individual therapy sessions; any of the range of Twelve-Step meetings on offer; meals in the canteen; and, for those inclined, quiet time in the meditation garden, a quaint scattering of cacti, pots of red and yellow flowers and carved stone benches. The highlight of the day was undoubtedly volleyball before sundown, which was the only time in the day, other than early morning, when it was comfortable to stay outside under the desert sun for more than five minutes.

Accommodation was in two-person bungalows. On arrival at The Lodge, I'd headed straight to mine for a lie-down, once I'd completed the obligatory medical examination and health check. Pushing open the door, I was met by a wall of ice-cold air. My roommate, who was apparently called Scott, was nowhere to be seen, so I turned the air-conditioner up to what I imagined would still be a chilly 18 degrees centigrade. There followed a proxy conversation through the air-con panel that stretched over the next 24 hours, as each of us kept returning to the room to find the other out, and the temperature not to his satisfaction. (Scott had come in that night to find me already in bed, feigning sleep, and I'd left in the morning before Scott was officially awake.) When we finally met, the scene was set for a confrontation, Lodge-style.

The confrontation formula went, 'When you did x, I felt y.' An optional suffix could be added: 'And what I made up about myself was z.' Confrontations became a matter of making others aware of how their actions affected you (in other words, guilt-tripping them) rather than the normal exchange of accusations that led nowhere. You were only allowed to use seven feelings: joy, shame, guilt, fear, loneliness, anger, and pain. Rather like primary colours, these were seen as the core feelings from which all other feelings derived; they were to be our emotional lingua franca at The Lodge. Roy encouraged us to include a core feeling with every share and modelled the use of the confrontation formula whenever the opportunity arose. I can still hear him saying in a flat voice to someone who'd arrived late to Blue Group, 'When you arrive late, I feel loneliness and pain.'

Anyway, I'd set the air con at 19 degrees, cool enough once it had time to kick in, then lay down on my bed and waited for Scott. I tried reading but couldn't keep my mind on the words. I kept going through my lines, 'When I woke up this morning to find the air-conditioning on high, I felt pain.' Pain in America, I'd discovered, meant emotional not physical pain. Or did I feel shame? Stick with pain. It didn't matter what feeling I chose as long as I went through with the process. I couldn't understand why I was so nervous. I'd confronted people before, though usually only when there seemed to be no other way or I'd blown my top. The phrasing of the formula certainly made you feel vulnerable; it forced you to offer up your feelings to the very person you felt had ignored them. Like Lars, Scott wanted you to know he was here to kick the juice, but they could keep the psychobabble. I rehearsed my suffix, 'And what I made up about myself was that you put your own comfort above mine.' Remember what Roy had said: make it about you and your feelings. 'What I made up about myself was that I didn't matter.'

I delivered my lines almost before Scott had got through the door. He fixed a patient look on his mouth and, waiting until I was quite sure I'd finished, replied in a bored tone that I'd been asleep so he didn't see how it mattered.

'Well it does,' I said, 'because now I've got a cold in the middle of a desert!'

He grunted and got into bed, leaving the temperature at 19 degrees. Result! But it took some getting used to, this speaking in formula.

At £3,000 a week, most people were at The Lodge on rehab-friendly American health insurance. The exceptions were the odd European such as myself and celebrities rich enough to be able to choose to avoid the potential exposure to the media that came with filling in a claim form. There was talk of this or that celebrity having checked in looking terrible but none was here at present. Not that The Lodge cared about celebrity status, of course. Not the film star kind anyway . . .

Dr Josh Spalding, international sex addiction guru, stopped by The Lodge once a month for one-to-ones with the newest intake of sex addicts. I'd half-expected to see the golden retriever, with whom he'd posed on the back of his bestselling book, lying beside his desk when I entered the room. He was in a navy cashmere blazer, charcoal slacks and open-necked sky-blue shirt. There was something Clintonian in the twinkle of his blue eyes and salt and pepper demi-bouffant.

We only had half an hour so I got down to business, sketching my "sexual history" from when I hid pellets of my shit behind a little hatch in my bedroom aged about three, through wearing other boys' woollen underwear, to "using" porn. I'd got so used to telling these anecdotes it felt like I was describing things to be proud of.

Spalding gave me my diagnosis: when I went to boarding school aged eight, I re-experienced the first time that I had been given away – by Alison. At the same time I discovered masturbation through the use of woollen underwear. This accidental meeting of a powerful need with an equally powerful solution sealed my fate as an underwear fetishist.

I bowed my head at the chiming of the words *underwear fetishist*. Here was another label I could call my own, fully sanctioned by the Great Man himself. I would tell Blue Group about it solemnly, make it seem as if I fully accepted Spalding's diagnosis. That should wind up Lars and a few other sex addiction-sceptics enough to make them try and convince me of the absurdity of the charge. 'But you stopped aged 13!' they'd plead, no doubt thinking about the labels Spalding could slap on them if he went that far back into their sexual histories.

'Well,' I'd sigh, not wanting to appear to let myself off too easily, 'I suppose: once an underwear fetishist, always an underwear fetishist.' After repeating the words underwear fetishist enough times, surely the whole group – maybe even Roy – would start seeing images of paunchy male CEOs in suspender belts, and the diagnosis would seem both too condemning and too light-hearted for my childhood experience.

What they wouldn't understand, and what I would not be foolish enough to explain, was that there was no way a Mulholland could ever be anything as *tacky* as an underwear fetishist. A tomcat between the sheets – yes. A cold-hearted Casanova – yes. But an underwear fetishist? Please.

Of course, I could see the hypocrisy in my position. I hid behind being a Mulholland when it suited me, while at the same time blaming how I felt on being a Mulholland. No doubt all children indulged in this mental back-flipping, even Rachel. Being adopted simply allowed me to do it with a greater zeal.

Spalding was smiling blankly at me: my thirty minutes were up. I thanked him for his time, saying he had given me a lot to think about and work on. He seemed gratified by this, which gratified me too. As long as he felt he had done a good job, I was happy. I'd played my part as supplicant sex addict. Now I could feel safe, a cog on the wheel of The Lodge, which was a cog on the wheel of the therapy industry, which was a cog on the wheel of post-lapsarian man.

As I scuttled out of his office, blinking into the fierce Arizona sun, I felt that I belonged. I knew that I didn't, but that was a mere detail by comparison.

I also knew I was no saint. The benefit of being at The

Lodge was that I'd finally found a place where I was demonstrably less screwed up than most other people. Here, I could see myself as the young mascot who leads his team onto the pitch at the beginning of a football match. I was the Innocent One. I could cast myself, in the words of King Lear, as 'a man more sinned against than sinning'. (And we all know what happens to King Lear by the end of the play.)

Spalding's take on the woollen underwear had been very much in line with The Lodge's position on addiction. No good came from looking beyond the surface of an addiction because all addiction was simply a way to numb emotional distress. Spalding and The Lodge believed that most patients were cross-addicted, meaning if they stopped abusing one thing, such as food, they would take up the slack with something else, such as sex. Only when the patient stopped "using" on all fronts could the real work of healing the original, usually childhood, wound begin. This was why they happily treated bulimics, heroin addicts and compulsive hand-washers in exactly the same way. They were all addicts trying to avoid, rather than face, unwelcome feelings.

I was paying The Lodge several thousand pounds a week, so I *wanted* to believe what they and their therapist-in-chief had to say. But I couldn't so easily brush aside the symbolism of wearing other boys' underwear. It had to represent more than an "accidental meeting" with a childhood trauma. I knew intuitively that underwear was wrapped up in the forming of my identity. It had to be about wanting to be somebody else, perhaps the popular, sporty biological child of my parents, perhaps the unadopted child of Alison who was so lovable and captivating that she had found it impossible to give me away.

Having recently completed a one-year introductory course in psychodynamic counselling, even I can sense an

Oedipal fixation in operation with the underwear fetishism. Clearly I was anxious about my role in the family unit and at boarding school. I was confused about how to express the overwhelming emotions and unconsciously linked all the confusion with being adopted.

The Lodge would no doubt reply, 'How would telling you that have helped you get your life back on track?'

In the end it came down to a client's preference, and I knew I needed a more symbolic approach. The good thing about being here though, was the openness. When I thought back to that eight-year-old boy, he would never in his worst nightmare have imagined *telling* anyone about the underwear. He fervently hoped and expected to carry all knowledge of the private James to the grave. He accepted that having a private and public self was a fact of life; although, oddly, he assumed other eight-year-olds had no such division. He was a freak, after all. But as long as he was a secret freak, where was the harm?

Sometimes I would be walking around The Lodge, saying 'Hi' to people I knew, and it would hit me: *They know.* They'd known about the underwear and they hadn't looked away in disgust, or rushed to fetch an orderly. In fact, in Blue Group it was the private James that drew people *to* me.

It could seem like alchemy, until you realised that it made perfect sense. I was beginning to realise that I may not be a certifiable freak after all. It was my defences (being distant, people-pleasing and self-sabotaging) that made me feel, in the words of an AA old-timer back in London, 'like an iceberg floating around in the sea'. My "sins", which the defences were meant to disguise, only looked so terrible from a child's point of view.

I was attending one of The Lodge's in-house Twelve-Step meetings, half-listening to someone share about the misery of their previous life, when I pictured myself aged eight. I can't remember where the young James was, probably in a neutral setting at Barton. I go up to the eight-year-old me, and give him a hug. He feels small in my arms and his hair smells of shampoo.

The viewpoint switches: I'm the young boy, looking up at the grown-up me. He's got soft eyes and he tells me I'm a lovely boy. He says he knows everything and it's fine, it's normal. There are tears in his eyes. He kisses the top of my head. I'm safe. I lean into him and don't want him to go.

*   *   *

The founder of the Lodge was the only other figure to equal Josh Spalding in hero status. An ex-nurse, she was apparently in recovery from love addiction and had written a number of books on the subject – pioneering, of course – that could be purchased at the centre's bookstore. According to legend, she would occasionally delight her flock by speaking at a soirée in startling detail about her past "acting out" behaviour. I thought I had glimpsed her once, getting into a big American car dressed in a white and gold tracksuit with a matching headband, looking like a middle-aged version of *The Kids from Fame*. But then a sniffy devotee told me I had probably seen one of her "clones".

There were local heroes too. Slim was a Vietnam vet always available for an informal chat, and Tad Poe was a clergyman who ran the Desert Experience, where a group of patients went out into the desert at night in their fourth week to act out rituals and make pledges. And there was Leo, a patient who, despite being clean from drugs for 15 years, returned every year in August for four weeks' treatment to, as someone told me admiringly, 'strengthen his recovery'. Recovery from what, he didn't say. But every morning Leo could be seen walking around the estate's boundary three times, his US Navy baseball cap pulled low over his forehead.

People were free to join him as they wished. One

morning he had so many needy patients around him he looked like Forrest Gump jogging across America. Apparently he was working on his "trauma bonds" this year. If there is a trace of cynicism in my tone it only reflects how envious I was of anyone projecting that much certainty.

My big breakthrough came on the volleyball court. Craig was a slight, prissy New Yorker in his thirties who had joined Blue Group a week after me. He let us know he'd been in recovery for some years and knew all the right words. If someone said something he felt was too graphic, such as 'blow job' or 'pussy', he would interrupt them saying it was 'inappropriate'. He was obsessed with the idea that the room had to be 'safe', as if we were a group of convent girls on a day out in Brighton. I think he may have reminded me of the shrimp Dave Farthing (Tiny) at Cranford by the way he hid behind words, although Dave had used his sharp tongue to pitch people against each other and then present himself as a mediator in an attempt to make himself indispensible, whereas Craig seemed determined to shut himself behind a wall of rules.

The same guy who peppered his shares with 'objectifying' and 'sexual relations', however, came out with perhaps the most graphic and disturbing anecdote I have ever heard in group counselling or Twelve-Step meetings. Craig would watch porno videos in the private cabins off Times Square, downing Starbucks triple shots and smoking Lucky Strikes. (These last details, I felt, intended to contrast favourably with the less sophisticated activities I'd confessed to taking part in during my university trip to Amsterdam.) Then one day he stuck a photograph of his mother on the partition wall of the cabin and walked out, leaving it there. You could see every other member of Blue Group take a little time to process that one. Nobody, not even Roy, seemed inclined to comment. The truth is there was something about Craig that reminded me of myself. A wary, needy little boy who cares only for his own invisibility, which he calls safety. And I didn't like the mirror he held up to me.

I was waiting for the other side of the volleyball court to serve when an arm pushed into my back. Craig, who was on my side, appeared to be trying to steer me into another part of the court. Before I could react, the ball came sailing over the net and I had to get on with playing. But I was niggled. I knew I'd have to confront him and that the "appropriate" time would be after the game.

For the rest of the set I fantasised about accidentally driving my elbow into his larynx or tripping over and crashing into his already-bandaged knee. I tried to decide if I felt pain at being pushed around like livestock, or shame at being such a wuss as to care. Then suddenly it hit me: I feel angry. Forget pain and shame, that's getting way too clever. I feel angry. When I told Scott I felt pain about the air-conditioning, that was bullshit: I felt angry. I've felt angry for years! Why haven't I been able to see it?

And in a flash I knew the answer: Because I saw anger as weakness, as impotence, even as insanity. I was the same as my father, both of us chose to step back and pretend nothing affected us. Better that, than join in my mother's raging. But I saw now that suppressing all that anger came at a price.

'When you pushed me in the back just then,' I told Craig, as we waited for some players to switch with those waiting to come on, 'I felt anger.'

He took a moment to take in what I was telling him, before saying, 'I'm sorry for pushing you.'

* * *

Only recently, eight years after returning from America, have I begun to realise that my parents didn't have to come for Family Week. I'd expected them to, because I blamed them for the mess I was in.

The Lodge tried to tell us there was a difference between blaming someone and holding them responsible. The former showed that you still saw yourself as a victim, defined by your past, while the latter indicated that you realised as an adult you were able to change your situation. Which was all very well in theory but you couldn't just switch your way of thinking because The Lodge told you to or because it made sense. I can see now, however, that my parents' decision to go to The Lodge shows how seriously they treated my situation; more seriously than I treated it.

The only version I could tolerate at the time was that my parents should come in order to face the music. I wanted them to suffer too, which was really a way of spreading out the seriousness of my situation, of playing down my part in it. If they were equally as messed up as me and they were doyens of Surrey society, all that was required was a redistribution of shit so that both parties had a manageable load to carry.

If that were really the case, they'd have been mad to come. But they interpreted the phone call by The Lodge's family liaison co-ordinator, inviting them to fly out for Family Week, correctly. They would be coming to help their son in his hour of need.

Alison, who was also asked, flew out with my parents, but they stayed at different hotels: my parents at a newly-constructed hotel beside a golf course, a good hour's drive from The Lodge, Alison at a more functional establishment in the nearby town. Legend has it the best part of the day was when both parties stopped at an ice-cream parlour on their way back to their respective hotels and treated themselves to whatever they fancied. They reckoned they deserved it!

Family Week kicked off with an introductory lecture on the principles of recovery as practised at The Lodge, followed by a group session. In Blue Group we sat in one large circle, patients next to their parents and partners, who wore name tags identifying the patient they were with. We went around the circle introducing ourselves. Everyone had to say who they were, what they were feeling, and ask for the group's support. When it came to Mummy she gave her name, said she was feeling apprehensive and hopeful, and asked for the group's support. Alison followed suit, and then Dad said, 'My name is Adrian. I feel sad but also hopeful. And I don't want the group's support.'

There was some shuffling in seats, before Roy inquired, 'Can I ask you why you don't want the group's support, Adrian?'

'Because I don't feel I need it. I've done perfectly well so far without it.'

I was, of course, annoyed with him. Wasn't he meant to be here for me? What was he trying to prove, he was the big City chairman who could take on all-comers single-handed? But even at the time I also admired his stand. I sensed that, at least subconsciously, Dad may have been sending me an important message: *Look, James, isn't always doing what people tell you at the heart of your problems? You'll gain much more by believing in yourself than filling the pockets of therapists in the hope of buying a miracle cure.*

Now, I see his refusal to play ball as the one funny moment in an otherwise humourless week. It is the only anecdote I tell about my time at The Lodge because, as well as guaranteeing a laugh, it so perfectly sums up my dad.

Roy, thankfully, saw there was no future in questioning my father further, at least at the present time, and we moved on to me. 'Name's James, sex addict, alcoholic, co-dependent. I'm feeling . . . blah, blah, blah.' Only now do I realise how disturbing this introduction must have been to my parents and Alison. They knew I'd been going to AA back home but not Sex Addicts Anonymous. No one as far as I was aware had briefed them on the broad definition of sex addiction within the therapeutic milieu. With only the front pages of tabloid newspapers for inspiration, they must have been wondering what heinous acts I'd be admitting to over the week. *Yes*, I was replying to Dad, *I will bring you all down to my level if I have to carry you kicking and screaming.*

My parents liked Lars's parents best because, being of Danish descent, they seemed the least American and therefore the most 'sensible'. Dad and Mummy were least impressed with Frank's elderly father, who'd come to make amends for 'fiddling with' Frank when he was a boy.

After the morning's work, Dad, Mummy, Alison and I had lunch together in the canteen. Patients and family were then separated for list work, in which we had to prepare a list of grievances we'd held against each other over the years. A few hours later, we met up again for refreshments. Mummy expressed her amazement at their counsellor Patsy, a thin, heavily made-up woman who'd told them she'd been married six times. 'I fail to see,' Mummy said, 'how someone who's gone through that many husbands can offer advice to anyone!'

I wasn't going to fall into the trap of explaining the role of counsellors, of defending The Lodge, especially as I found Patsy a bit spooky myself, so I laughed, and we all hugged *au* Lodge, and off they sped towards their waiting sundaes, followed by stiff gin and tonics once they'd reached the hotel.

The delivering of lists, considered the centrepiece of Family Week, begins on Thursday morning. Under the supervision of a specially trained family counsellor, each party reads their grievances to the person concerned. Grievances are meant to be specific, clear and concise, after which the recipient has the opportunity to 'make amends' if they feel it is appropriate, or simply acknowledge that they have heard and understood what the other person has said. Families are kept together whenever possible so that everyone can hear all parties' grievances.

This way, the theory goes, subtle manipulations of the truth are less likely to be attempted. After all, the family is a dynamic organism, so each member ought to be privy to shifts that will affect them all. In the case of Alison, however, our family counsellor Sarah agreed to let Alison and me have a separate session from my one with Mummy and Dad, which suited us all fine. Nonetheless, it was a curious granting of dispensation by an institution that prided itself on facing down anything thrown at it.

Sarah and I had privately agreed it would be 'appropriate' and beneficial for all concerned if, at the start of my *in camera* list work with Mummy and Dad, I were to share about the pellets of shit and woollen underwear. I didn't say to Sarah, 'After all, they practically qualify as pleasantries here!' She took it all very seriously, which I was flattered by and I didn't want to break the spell. Of course, my hidden agenda – that I didn't care to admit even to myself – was to get *my parents* to pick up the shit and wear the woollen underwear for a while. See how they liked it.

The two memorable points in Mummy's list were my not wearing a suit at Dad's recent seventieth birthday party, which I apologised for, and my snapping at her while Dad was in hospital awaiting surgery. The two of us had been sitting in the lounge of their London flat when it'd happened. I'd had some whiskeys and she asked me if I'd be 'the man of the house' until Dad had recovered. I replied in a defensive tone that I did not want to take on that role.

I can remember thinking that my mother hadn't held back in drawing up her list, and being glad she was willing to give the process a go. I decided to apologise for the way I'd spoken to her in the flat but not for the answer I'd given. Now I think I was ungenerous, both at the time of Dad's surgery and at The Lodge. Rather than thinking about her plight and agreeing to a request that was hardly something I would have had to demonstrate in any concrete way, I'd chosen to think about the psycho-sexual implications of becoming my (adoptive) mother's 'man'. At The Lodge I'd told myself it had been my father who was ill, as well as her husband, so why shouldn't I be upset and behave erratically too? Again, I had a point, but it wasn't exactly being supportive in her hour of need. Where was the caring, or at least chivalrous, son in all this?

My list to Mummy contained examples of times she'd, as I saw it, shamed me during my childhood. I told her the thing I'd hated most was being told to stop showing off. I'd be getting carried away doing something goofy or talking on and on, milking the grownups' attention, and then she'd tell me to stop showing off. It was as if my clothes had instantly vanished and I was standing naked in front of everyone, a pink quivering blob of neediness.

Mummy apologised for the words she'd chosen but said, to be fair, she'd probably told me ten times already to stop doing whatever it was I was doing and had run out of ways of getting me to do as I was asked.

Touché: she was apologising for the way she'd spoken to me, but not for what she'd meant, just as I'd done with her list.

I also included in my list how mortified I had been when she'd shouted at Rachel and me, particularly in front of our friends. Sarah had told me I needed to include some specific examples but I said Mummy would only claim she didn't remember the incident, and in so doing discredit the overall grievance. In the end we agreed I'd cite a particular holiday we'd spent in my parents' property in the South of France when Rachel and I were in our late teens. The party had included two of my parents' friends, the couple's son, and friends invited by Rachel and me. We had a boat at our disposal, swimming, sun and fabulous French food, but Mummy kept flying off the handle at the smallest thing. 'Stop treating the place like a hotel!' she'd shout at our friends and me because we were sitting down while something needed doing. In the end, whenever Mummy appeared everyone stood up as if she were the Queen.

When I told Mummy this list item, she thought about it for a moment and said, 'It must have been awful growing up frightened of your mother.' I didn't know what to say. It sounded almost as if she were talking about someone else, and yet I could see in her eyes that she felt a deep sadness about it. Suddenly I wanted to take it all back. *Every mother loses her temper*, I wanted to say. *I shouldn't have made such a big deal about it.* But I decided not to say anything, figuring I was probably being swept along by a passing eddy of guilt.

Dad, needless to say, did not follow the list rubric. Instead of citing specific grievances, he made general comments about the way my life had turned out thus far. He said he thought that in my third year at university my attitude had changed and I hadn't seemed happy any more. I thought back: that would be when I started going out with Mary, my first ever girlfriend. Her East Coast liberal American view had stirred up something in me, a questioning side. Surrey and Cranford had no longer seemed like the only ways to see the world.

Dad then said he was sad I hadn't got a book published, and regretted encouraging me down that road.

It was a list of sadness and regret and I found it hard to listen to. It brought home why I was really here: I hadn't made anything of my life. The main thing I wanted to get off my chest to Dad was his standing by while Mummy raged. A specific grievance I had concerned an occasion in my late teens when Dad and I had had a hushed conversation in the hall of our Surrey home after Mummy had been shouting at us. He said he'd spoken with a surgeon friend of theirs who knew Mummy well and the surgeon had said there was nothing any of us could do about Mummy's temper because she was 'mentally unwell' at the time.

I told Dad that on the one hand I'd seen this as him legitimising doing nothing, and yet I'd also felt real fear (Was our family unravelling?) as well as frustration (Did that mean we had to put up with this indefinitely?).

Once I'd finished speaking, Dad looked me straight in the eye and said he'd never said that.

It felt like I'd been slapped in the face. I couldn't believe he would betray his own son in his hour of need to save his own skin.

Since that moment, the more I look back on that hushed conversation in the hall, the less I can be 100 per cent sure about the accuracy of my recollection. Was I *certain* he'd used the all important word 'mentally'? Yes, but *not 100 per cent*. Might he have said 'not well mentally'? He may have done, but I don't think he did.

Had it *definitely* been in the hall? Yes. I *think* so.

This kind of thought process could get scary. It was one thing having your interpretations queried, quite another having the validity of your memories questioned. After all, who is a person other than a collection of sensory, cognitive and emotional memories?

From my father's point of view, however, I can see now that there was only one response he could have made: deny it if he remembered saying it; deny it if he thought he might have said it; deny it if he was certain he hadn't said it. His justification: how could one conversation ten years ago, uttered under stress or not uttered at all, have any noticeable effect on my rehabilitation? Whereas the level of aggravation resulting from openly betraying his wife must have seemed well worth avoiding. Seen from that light, it was I who had betrayed Dad by bringing it up in the first place.

Alison and my lists were a low key affair by comparison. She hadn't liked the way I'd complained to her that her husband Davy didn't understand my adoption dilemma, after he'd listened so carefully to what I'd had to say on the matter. If I forced her to make a choice between Davy or me, she told me, she'd choose her husband. Melodramatic delivery, I thought, but I got her point. Then it was my turn and I fired a half-hearted shot across her bows concerning an occasion when I'd been driving us somewhere in Cornwall and she'd criticised me for not waving thank you to another driver for letting me in. My heart wasn't in my list with Alison. I felt I'd already done the big stuff with my parents. A few years down the line, it would have been different. Then I might have said, 'When you gave me a lesson in driving etiquette, I felt like saying "I don't think I need to be taught manners from someone who gave me away to strangers".' But I'd only just discovered being angry at Craig, nice controllable anger with a beginning and an end. Finding, let alone venting, my anger at Alison was still some way off.

We parted on the Friday afternoon, exchanging weak smiles. *What had all this washing of dirty linen in public gained?* my parents and Alison clearly wondered. How could that process have rejuvenated my sagging self-confidence? But they *had* done what they could. Yes, they had, and the gratitude I was already feeling grated against my official version of why they'd come – to share the shit.

I desperately wanted to be driving back to my parents' hotel, then tucking into a gin and tonic on the balcony, eyeing the female golfers as they prepared to swing their clubs. But no, you see I was an alcoholic and sex addict. There would be no more of that kind of depravity. I watched them drive off in their metallic green rental Ford, and told myself that love, however it was served – and who was I to stand in judgement of love? – was superior to the best theories in the world, even those wrapped in £3,000 a week paper with a bow around them.

* * *

Roy considered that I was too raw to go back into the

outside world after four weeks of "psychological surgery" at The Lodge and persuaded me to check into Balfore Place, a "halfway house" on the east coast of America. He said he had 'very real concerns about my readiness to reintegrate', and that Balfore Place would give me the chance to acclimatise slowly to the temptations and rigours of the outside world. I did wonder if there was a kickback involved, but booked a place anyway. I reasoned to myself that I did feel wobbly, and at £1,200 a week it was a snip compared with The Lodge.

There was also the fact that I had no job, no girlfriend and a dusty home in Twickenham awaiting me should I opt to fly straight back to England.

It didn't take me long to fit into life at Balfore Place. Housed in a four storey red brick mansion in a leafy suburb, it was both halfway in terms of the freedom given to clients (not "patients", as we were called at The Lodge), and in terms of culture, being halfway between the zany earnestness of Arizona and conservative, cynical Britain.

I arrived just in time for dinner, which was self-service from trays delivered by the centre's sister hospital a few blocks away. Most chores around the house, I discovered, were completed by the clients in accordance with rotas pinned to a notice-board beside me. Jobs ranged from taking out the rubbish, to cleaning communal rooms, chairing the nightly Twelve-Step meeting, and washing up and laying out the cutlery before meals. Every client around the table was male, in his twenties or thirties, and most seemed as animated as schoolboys, joshing each other and keen to explain the workings and idiosyncrasies of Balfore Place and its staff. It was as if I'd been sent to a second, alternative public school in order to finish the emotional education I'd never received at Cranford.

Within a few days at Balfore Place, I could look back on The Lodge with a mix of irony and amazement. It had been like being a baby again. I'd even carried a teddy around, to represent my Wounded Child.

In The Lodge everything came to you. Food was provided, therapy was provided, a volleyball court, ball and opponents were provided, and parents and partners flew out to you at Family Week. Whenever you screamed or cried there was someone there to interpret your needs and calm your fears. Even the mattress had a plastic cover. But there was only so much you could take of it. Every child wanted to grow up. Moving to Balfore Place, it was as if I'd become a teenager. I was excited to explore and rebel, within clearly set boundaries.

The clients at Balfore Place were the friendliest, funniest, most self-destructive guys you could fit into one house at a time without the roof blowing off. If our main therapist, Bernard, an expert in treating Vietnam Veterans suffering from Post-traumatic Stress Disorder, had thought he was coming here for an easy time, he'd presumably changed his mind quicker than a GI's napalm flashback.

I shared a room with a gentle, sandy haired fellow called George, whose "MO" – I later found out this was short for *modus operandi* – was "object sex". Believing his office in a department store to be empty, he'd been impaling himself on a chair leg one day when a colleague had returned to pick up something she'd left behind.

Todd, who was the youngest of us and Bernard's pet, would be getting on fine in his life, and the next moment he'd be going up to a strange girl he'd seen on the street or in a store, trying to arrange a date with her and refusing to take no for an answer. He already had a long list of harassment complaints. It was clear he never touched them or threatened them with violence but, as he readily, shamefacedly admitted, his behaviour was threatening.

'Amen to that,' Ralf, a podgy, balding Peeping Tom would say empathetically. He was here because one day the owners of a house whose French windows he was peering through heard something and turned on the lawn lights.

There he was, hand around his todger, blinking into the white beam as if posing for a photograph. We were all amazed when, several weeks after first hearing the story, he let it be known that the people inside the house had been fully dressed. He found cosy family scenes irresistible.

Denny, from Florida, was built like an American footballer, had a pockmarked face and was a talented musician as well as running a successful recording studio. But when he got the itch he would go on a cocaine-fuelled prostitution bender in Tampa Bay's red light district that could last days. Worse was to come: by the end of the bender his knob would be bruised and bleeding and, more than likely, he still hadn't managed to come.

But Balfore Place's star turn was surely Carla. A trim Puerto Rican transsexual, Carla wore jeans and vaguely feminine tops and looked, as far as I was concerned, like a camp gay bloke. She had a teasing way with us males, talking laddishly about sport, cars or whatever and then, when you least expected it, turning all coy. Her *pièce de résistance* was waiting for enough newcomers to arrive and then sharing the story of her operation. 'Ee wasen painfool a'all,' she'd say. 'Zay geev you as mush morphine as you lie, an zen I ad my own crack.' The best bit was saved until last, when she'd say deadpan, 'I geev my farzer my balls een ah glass jar, has a birthday geef.' One day I went down to breakfast and she'd vanished. The manager of Balfore Place sent out one of his trainee counsellors to the downtown area to see if she could be found around the crack houses, but to no avail.

Every house has to have its scapegoat, its dropout, its Thle. Ours was a cherub-faced paedophile called Kevin who looked like he was in his late twenties. Bernard, like all trendy teachers, allowed and even encouraged our alternating prodding and ignoring of Kevin, no doubt sensing an easy way to ensure the rest of the group gelled under a common enemy. We never learnt what Kevin did other than follow young boys. It crossed my mind, judging by the aloof relish with which he accepted the role of scapegoat, that he may not have been a paedophile at all, or only one in his head. Perhaps a part of him had decided it was the only role that did justice to the truly terrible person that he believed he was.

When he left – or we'd got rid of him – Bernard admitted he had a young child living in the area and couldn't stand the thought of Kevin roaming the streets. We sympathised, but all sensed, I think, that the spotlight would now be searching our own dark sides.

Nevertheless I felt confident that, as at The Lodge, my "offending behaviour" – the name given to our predilections here – would scrub up well beside those of my peers. How bad was nicking underwear as a child, compared to harassing women in the street as an adult? I knew that I just had to come to terms with my past, whereas the rest of them were liable to leave Balfore Place and go straight out and "re-offend". As at The Lodge, I wanted to have the best of both worlds: to bond with flawed people while at the same time feeling superior to them. I didn't get away with it for long.

Bernard, who had an adopted daughter, treated me softly on the whole. I was grateful for this at the time, although I sensed I was being let off the hook, which might not be good for me in the long run. How he helped me instead, however, was literally to build me up. He valued what I had to say. And as a result, the rest of the group did too. I knew that I was an integral part of the team. To this day, I am grateful to him for that.

But it took a gestalt therapist, who visited once a week from the sister hospital, to nail me down. Someone was sharing about their heavy duty offending behaviour and then I started talking about the dusty house in Twickenham that I would soon be . . .

'When are you going to get out of your woollen

underwear and join the rest of us?' the therapist asked me in a neutral voice.

I looked at him aghast. I couldn't think what to say. I felt as if I were sitting in front of everyone dressed only in a St Michael woollen vest and pants.

Finally the cavalry arrived. *How dare you refer to my sexual history in that way!* I thought, flames of self-righteous rage burning my chest, demanding that I defend my honour. 'When am I?...' I tried. 'What?... But...' I looked around the circle at the other faces: George, Denny, Ralf, Sean, Ingemar, Carla. Each was watching intently, but none would give me even so much as a sympathetic grimace. I was alone.

And in the group at last. Because no matter how different our reasons for coming here might appear, the overriding thing that these reasons had in common was they'd brought us to our knees.

At the time I had no idea that a raft of studies existed, mostly based in America, showing that adoptees are significantly overrepresented in psychiatric hospitals and treatment centres. In his 1993 report on the long-term effects of adoption, Brodzinsky states, 'Findings from a [US] health household survey of parents are especially relevant to the question of psychological risk associated with adoption. At eleven to seventeen years of age, children adopted in infancy were 2.5 times more likely than non-adopted youngsters to have ever received professional help from a psychiatrist or psychologist and over three times more likely to have received or needed such help in the past year.'

The figures for all adoptees, not just those adopted in infancy, are of course higher still. According to Brodzinsky, a large-scale health survey in the US found that although adoptees make up two per cent of children under eighteen years of age, they constitute approximately five per cent of children referred to outpatient mental health clinics and, on average, between ten and fifteen per cent of children in residential care homes and psychiatric hospitals.

It is interesting to speculate how many other adoptees were at The Lodge and Balfore Place during my stays at each. It would seem likely that I was not the only one making a show of wrestling with various "addictions", while our real issue – adoption – went largely unexplored by counsellors and ourselves alike. Unfortunately, almost no data exists on *adult* adoptees who seek psychological help in all its guises, so one can only guess at the true long-term impact of adoption.

Possibly the biggest reason why Balfore Place was such an enjoyable and helpful place for me was the friendship I formed with Malcolm. A Welshman, Malcolm had moved to LA to work in the film industry, had married an American, and stayed. He was in rehab because around once a week he'd draw the blinds in his office after everyone had left and watch porn, snort coke and drink Jack Daniels until daylight started creeping between the slats and he realised he'd been at it for ten hours. We became best friends in the schoolboy sense of the word. We were always together and we never stopped talking, whether sitting in each other's room listening to music, playing table tennis on the veranda or strolling under the statuesque New England trees, whose fall leaves were every shade of gold and brown imaginable. The only way our friendship may have differed from best mates at school was we told each other everything, filtered nothing and trusted each other completely.

Once a week we all got into the centre's van and were driven to Borders bookstore, where we experimented with interacting with the outside world for an hour or so. What did you feel as you walked past Erotic Fiction? What did you feel as the female shop assistant handed you your plastic bag of books? What did you feel as you sat in the coffee shop sipping *latte* like anyone else?

Todd made sure he was always with a "buddy", but one time Todd gave him the slip when the buddy was having a pee and was next seen walking beside a harassed-looking woman in the car park, gesturing with his hands like an Italian waiter.

After the Borders excursion we would go to a Sex Addicts Anonymous meeting nearby. Held in a large brightly lit room in the municipal building, around forty chairs would already be set out in a circle, leaving space at one end for those who arrived early to stand around drinking coffee, socialising. The atmosphere couldn't have been further from the cold, damp crypt in London that I'd cut my SAA teeth on. Here you felt that when the clock struck eight, everyone could as easily begin rehearsing *Annie Get Your Gun* as take their seats for a Sex Addicts Anonymous meeting. There was no shame; for better, largely, but maybe sometimes also for worse.

The one person whose attendance Balfore Place held our collective breath for was Jeanine, a pale buxom undergraduate who anywhere else wouldn't have turned a head, but in here, with her SAA manual in its homemade cloth jacket with lace trim placed demurely on her lap, she was our Botticelli's Venus. When it came to splitting into groups for personal sharing, it was like watching a bad spy film. Guys pretended to have wandered by chance into her group, even as it swelled disproportionately.

And Jeanine delivered, talking shyly about how she would find herself touching herself in a crowded elevator or watch herself making flagrant passes at her married boss, and feel so *out of control*. I can remember looking slyly at her fingers, which had short-clipped nails, picturing . . .

You're objectifying, a voice in my head would tell me and I'd force myself to stare at a framed photograph on the wall of an Amish family riding in a buggy with fields of corn either side of them – until she'd finished sharing.

On the way back we'd chant the Serenity Prayer

203

together: 'God grant me the serenity to accept the things I cannot change, courage to change the things I can, and wisdom to know the difference.' Each of us would share our recent experiences and feelings (Todd saying he'd learnt no place was safe, even the Mind, Body and Spirit aisle in Borders – 'Especially the Mind, Body and Spirit aisle!' the rest of the van chorused) and then we'd stop at a petrol station to buy ourselves a treat.

After eight weeks of laughter, friendship and honesty, I felt revived inside, ready to face my dusty flat. I vowed that I would move house to be nearer my friends and Twelve Step meetings, take a stopgap job while I looked into retraining and, fingers crossed, find a girlfriend.

8
Joy

I met Don McCleod, my birth father, in the reception of the Strand Palace Hotel at 2pm on a Saturday in April. 'Is that . . .?'

'Is that . . .?'

We shook hands. He had thinning sandy hair, a rugged, possibly boozy face and a round stomach that filled his tan shirt like a sack of corn. Walking shoes, dark chinos, weathered Barbour jacket; outdoorsy, then.

We had tea in the hotel café, a colonial-look interior with wicker chairs and tropical plants. He told me he had two children, a boy aged 23 (in media after graduating from Cambridge), and a girl aged 21 (currently at Durham University). He said he rarely rang them and wasn't the kind of father who believed in handouts. 'In short,' he seemed to be saying, 'if you're thinking of leaning on me, forget it; a) my children are more successful than you, and b) I'm not even interested in *them*.'

I asked him, *en passant*, if they knew about me.

He assured me they did not, then asked me what I did for a living.

'Nothing,' I said. This was *not* how the role-play of

meeting my birth father had gone at Balfore Place, with Bernard playing Don McCleod. We'd made all kinds of links then, tears in our eyes. But all this guy wanted to do was get shot of me – for a second time, I reminded myself. If anyone was going to walk out, it should be me!

I decided to go for the jugular: 'Does' – I was going to say *Mrs McCleod*, but it would sound too sarcastic – 'your wife know about me?'

Don said that she did not. He didn't even try to hide his discomfort at this revelation. Gathering himself admirably, however, he enquired what a chap like me, who looked healthy and was obviously intelligent, was doing without a career.

'It all goes back to being adopted,' I said.

He shrugged, as if to say, *It's your life to waste.*

I can remember looking at the contour of his lips, which would be mine in twenty years, and thinking that the words passing between them were as bleak and cumbersome as a line of tankers leaving a depot. How would I retell this afternoon to my mate Adam? He'd been so enthusiastic about today's meeting, so touched when I'd asked him to help me find my birth father. He'd looked through the licence database at the BBC where he worked, and printed out the address of every D. McCleod in the country. We sent letters to all 30 of them.

It had been Adam's idea to begin the letter: 'I am writing on behalf of a friend who is trying to trace a long-lost relative,' giving his Streatham home as the return address. This way the approach would seem less forceful and I'd be protected should Don McCleod wish to contact me in the future, against my wishes. We hadn't been able to believe it when the correct Don McCleod turned out to be the one who lived nearest, in Dulwich.

I almost felt more disappointed for Adam than myself with the way the meeting seemed to be turning out. When it came to telling him all about it, I'd have to make it sound either better or worse than it was, at least make it entertaining. *McCleod's defences lowered as our colonial rendezvous progressed,* I rehearsed to myself. *He ordered cake to go with a second cup of tea.*

Don did seem more at ease than when we'd first started talking. Perhaps he was beginning to realise I wasn't after his money. I began to feel sorry for the guy, knowing the dilemma he'd leave here with. If he told his wife about me she'd want to know why he'd kept it a secret throughout their marriage, and if he didn't tell her he ran the risk that I would. It was a nice idea, his wife answering the door, me going: 'Name's James, sex addict, alcoholic, son of Don McCleod.'

We chattered about sport for a bit and I asked him what it had been like playing water polo for England. When Don replied that he had only ever played for a local club, we agreed with a joint chuckle – the comic high point of our meeting – that Alison must have exaggerated on the adoption forms in order to make me sound like a better prospect. Either that, I thought, or you made it up at the time to impress her.

We parted with handshakes, exchanging phone numbers and saying we'd get together again soon. *So he's made his decision*, I remember thinking. *Now I've got to decide if I want us to meet again.* There didn't seem much to be gained or lost, I realised with a full sense of anticlimax.

Since returning from America my interactions with my parents had returned to normal, which was wary, with an extra irritant thrown in. Now whenever I rang, the first thing Dad would ask was if I'd found a job. I wanted to tell him I'd moved house; engaged a new therapist (a Jungian psychoanalyst whom Bernard had recommended after hearing him speak at a conference in America); adopted two cats – in an ironic twist, I would end up giving both back to the pet shelter once I realised their only interest in me was as a provider of beef or chicken Iams; and read x number of books on therapy while all the time maintaining a punishing regime of Twelve-Step meetings. But for Dad, the success of my American interlude and the months of therapy before and after could be judged according to one simple criterion: *Is the guy any closer to gaining meaningful employment?* And, deep down, I knew he was right – eventually I would have to take the plunge and *join in.*

Soon after meeting Don I went down to my parents' Surrey home for dinner. Dad asked if I had a job yet, Mummy started on about the "cracked" – for which read "gravely flawed" – staff at The Lodge, and I announced that I'd met Don McCleod, my birth father. Dad's eyes moistened and he said he was pleased. I told them all about the meeting, making Don sound marginally livelier than he was, which wasn't hard. I left Dad in no doubt, however, that he had nothing to fear from Grizzly Don. 'He didn't even play water polo for England!' I finished with a whoop.

Dad opened a celebratory half bottle of champagne, as I remember, and, lining up three flutes, poured a glass for Mummy and himself and an Aqua Libra for me. We toasted "us", and then, perhaps because therapy-speak had become second nature to me, perhaps because I was making trouble, I asked him, 'Don't you feel threatened?'

'Not at all,' Dad replied.

I could see he meant it. *Ten thousand dads*, his mournful eyes told me, *aren't going to help you land a job.*

Don told his wife, and I met up with his family for Sunday lunch in their Dulwich home. Talk centred around university life and current affairs. My birth father, I realised, was a straightforward man who'd got himself in a fix but had faced up to what he'd done and not done and had tried to make them right. His wife, Sue, was open and hospitable, going to the trouble of preparing a roast with trimmings and a homemade pudding. And his children, Alastair and Ginnie, were keen to get to know me. If, through their magnanimity, their father's fall from grace should be thrown into sharper relief so much the better. Or was that lowering others to my level?

I remember noticing that Ginnie was cute and aware, and wondering what might have been if I'd met her without knowing who she was. I also remember noticing that Alastair was shorter than me and deciding that, irrespective of whether he'd rowed for his college at Cambridge, I could beat him up if it came to that. (The last time I'd been in an actual fight, I hasten to add, had been on a dormitory floor when I was 14 years old.) Then it occurred to me that I was at a Sunday lunch in leafy Dulwich and our relative statuses would not be decided by sex and violence. Our statuses would not be decided at all. Nothing would be decided. Because this was real life, where everyone else had priorities and dilemmas as important to them as mine were to me. Ginnie would notice me eyeing her across her college bar at Durham and think, *I hope that pensioner doesn't come over and try to chat me up.* And Alastair would see me getting worked up during a future get-together in a pub, drain his pint and say cheerio.

In fact, I would not meet either of my "biological siblings" again (as this book goes to press). All would be left grey and murky, which is as it should be. Because, I realised after the Sunday lunch, I didn't *need* the McCleods. I didn't *need* Alison. I was committed to my relationship with her and, despite some recent phone calls in which suspicion had crackled in the background like gunfire behind a reporter in a war zone, I liked her. I even loved her, the "even" inserted to allow me to make a stronger statement, by omitting the word, about my adoptive mother who has always been my real mother. ("Real" is sometimes used to refer to the birth parent but in my opinion it is the perfect term for the adoptive mother, who has experienced the day-to-day reality of bringing up the child.)

Now that Sue had appeared, it seemed more important

than ever to rank, in my mind, my mothers and new "birth stepmother". I imagined Mummy would want this too, though no doubt it was more for myself. Besides, I was male so I was genetically programmed to make lists where females didn't see the necessity (top fifty films), and to forget them when they had been made especially for me by my wife (shopping).

Both birth parents had been stones I had to turn over to see what was underneath. And by any standard, I'd been lucky with what I'd found there. But above all, it had been the turning over – the rite of passage – that had been important. The people I had actually met were not my birth parents frozen in time for 29 years, and I was no longer the baby they had given away. The hole in my identity could not be filled by this middle-aged woman and man.

I am reminded of the central metaphor in Robert Bly's book on contemporary men's issues, *Iron John*. Relocating the Grimm fairytale 'Iron Hans' in a modern context, Bly describes how the Prince must free the Wild Man from his cage by stealing the key from under the Queen's pillow. The Prince represents the innocent boy that every male begins life as, the Wild Man is his inner masculine strength and the Queen is his mother. To become a man, the Prince must move out of his mother's protection. It is not for her to push him away; it is for him, with the help of the Wild Man inside, to wrench himself apart from her. He must risk *disobeying* her and consequently *losing her affection*. Here Bly is focusing on the Oedipal love between mother and son that must be outgrown. In Western culture today, the key is typically stolen considerably later than the Freudian ideal of five years old, often happening when a man marries, but it could occur earlier as a rebellious teenager or it could never take place. For me, it happened when I told Mummy that I had met Alison. (I do not take the *Iron John* metaphor to mean, as some would have it, that you must reject the mother and her values in order to become a man. Rather, you must unattach from the mother in order to be in a position to appreciate her values freely.)

*   *   *

My psychoanalysis was taking me in a different direction from the principles of AA and SAA. I began to see the labels of alcoholic or sex addict as counter-productive; they'd always seemed that way from my analyst's Jungian perspective. I stopped going to Twelve-Step meetings regularly. Until one summer evening, sitting in Adam's garden, I popped the cap off a bottle of ice cold Corona. In a few days I was back to the 'two to three whiskeys or the equivalent on weekdays, four to five on weekends' and 'occasional use' of porn that had got me certified by Beth Madison as an alcoholic and sex addict respectively. And I was not bundled into the back of a police van with a blanket over my head.

I stopped all meetings of any kind soon afterwards and enrolled on a PGCE. Not that I'd always wanted to be a teacher, but my analyst told me I had to do something and teaching was the kind of profession you could enter aged 31 without anyone caring too much what you'd failed to achieve in your twenties.

No more special and odd. That was what I was aiming for. Over the next eight years, how I began to feel like a real teacher, taking professional pride in my craft, and how I married a beautiful, fascinating, caring woman is another story. But I will relate two anecdotes, one about teaching and the other about marrying Elizabeth, because they provide a link between the previous pages of this memoir and the present.

Much of a PGCE is spent on work placement, where your lessons are observed by a mentor, ideally an experienced teacher within the department. My mentor for my first school placement had gained her PGCE the previous year; Deidre was young, black and feisty. After my first lesson, the two of us adjourned for debriefing to the Head of Department's study, a glass box in one corner to the humanities staff room. Deidre proceeded to list all the things I'd done wrong. I bristled, voices were raised. The next thing I knew, the Head of Department was informing me I had to report to a tribunal the following day, where Deidre's complaint could be formally heard in front of a member of the senior management team.

Fortunately I had my weekly appointment with my analyst Leonard that evening. I flopped down on the couch and relayed to him what had happened. 'The Head of Department was also female and black,' I concluded, and they'd ganged together to put that white jumped-up public school boy in his place. It was payback time!

'Who are you to criticise these people to their faces!' Leonard cut in fiercely. 'Your mentor and Head of Department! Hard-working professionals trying to help you become a teacher – my God!'

It was like I was falling through space. I'd never felt such shame. All the therapists I'd come into contact with so far had been encouraging, effusive, even the gestalt therapist at Balfore Place who'd asked me when I was going to get out of the woollen underwear and join the rest of them, had been clearly trying to provoke a reaction from me. None had shown anger, let alone disgust, towards me. None had *disliked* me, which was the hardest to take.

It was a turning point. Leonard had got through the protective shield that said I was only a teacher as part of my rehabilitation, that really I was something infinitely greater, yet to be discovered. He made me see I was far from being even a teacher, let alone the finest young writer of the second half of the twentieth century, raconteur and heroic survivor of adoption. He told me this was my last chance and I better go to the tribunal tomorrow with a better attitude or they'd have me slung out. I was on my own now, I realised, outside the orbit of Dad's money and Mummy's social graces.

I went in the next day like a whipped puppy and was given a formal warning, which I had to sign in the presence of witnesses. Years later when Leonard and I revisited the occasion during analysis, he admitted that Deidre and the Head of Department may have had racial, class and/or gender issues with me but that had been beside the point at the time. The chance to deflate me had been too good to waste by taking a balanced view.

When I meet that airy nonchalance in someone now, that forgery of confidence – public school or not – it is like looking into a ghastly mirror. Of course I want every student that crosses my path to like me, love me; I'm a teacher after all. We can't help it. But I'd rather drive home wrestling with whether Rob or Laura hates me or was just in a bad mood when they blanked me in the corridor, than never have entered the ring in the first place.

The second anecdote concerns our wedding day. Sadly, Davy had passed away, so Alison was accompanied by Lorna. In a gesture typical of my mother's generosity and appreciation of symbolism, she had asked if Alison could sit in the font aisle of the church alongside the immediate family. Elizabeth, my wife-to-be, and I had agreed.

Ever since I'd first met Alison in Cornwall, she had said she would like to sing *Ave Maria* during the signing of the marriage certificate if I were to 'find someone special' one day. But when it came to deciding the format of the service, everyone involved agreed it would be best if she didn't sing then. Alison was relieved, saying she would have done it for me but it would have been an awful pressure.

It would also have been symbolically wrong – from my perspective, anyway. I did not want the day to be a celebration of how far an adopted person could come with the help of a loving bride, supportive parents and an open-hearted birth mother (not to mention years of psychoanalysis). Of course, that impression could never be completely eradicated. As I stood at the altar, waiting for Elizabeth to arrive, I caught myself thinking, Is this really happening to *me*? Am I *enough*?

But no doubt most grooms think similar thoughts. Getting married is one of the biggest decisions you'll make, second perhaps only to having children. And making such a solemn, public commitment just seems so *grown-up*. It would be strange, in fact worrying, if the groom wasn't a bit anxious.

I have to keep reminding myself that there is no such thing as an adopted person, only a person who is adopted. I was given up for adoption not because there was something wrong with me.

The other thing I'll say with regard to getting married is that I doubt it would have been possible without first meeting Alison, or at least making every effort to find my birth mother; and without psychoanalysis.

Alison lurked behind my two previous girlfriends, making it impossible for me to commit. How could I commit to a girl when I didn't know where I came from – why I was here at all, and when I feared that she might suddenly want to get rid of me for no good reason?

And the psychoanalysis has kept me from sabotaging the good things that I have been allowing into my life. What a seemingly bland statement to make about seven years of crossing London every Tuesday evening for a double session of psychic surgery. Bland but true. For there have been no eureka moments when I have finally been able to release ancient pent-up feelings. I no longer even believe in such psychic poos that once expulsed make you feel a stone lighter.

In fact, I doubt whether feelings can be stored in this way. More likely, responses to experiences are stored, and when something similar occurs, they are reactivated, triggering feelings. It is therefore the old responses that need to be relived on the psychoanalytic couch, seen as outmoded and upgraded to an adult version. Feelings are not the end of the road. They are to be respected but not – as I feel was encouraged at The Lodge – worshipped as ends in themselves.

It is the eureka attitude to feelings that appears to underpin Attachment Therapy, a dangerous practice that a number of adopted children in America have fallen victim to. Attachment therapists claim a 90 per cent success rate in treating Reactive Attachment Disorder (RAD), where a sufferer finds it difficult or is unable to form attachments in early life. They advertise themselves as 'specialists in adoption issues', attracting adoptive parents who want to 'do adoption right'.

Attachment Therapy holds that the negative emotions of a child must be "released" for a child to function normally. Most controversial is their employment of "holding therapy", where a child is wrapped in a blanket and laid on by up to five adults. Tragically, at least four children have died while undergoing Attachment Therapy. The most publicised case was of ten-year-old adoptee Candace Newmaker, whose Attachment therapist, Connell Watkins, was jailed for 16 years for "reckless child abuse" in 2001. According to *The Rocky Mountain News*, Candace was 'wrapped tightly in a navy blue flannel sheet. Eight large pillows were then placed around her, while Watkins [and three others] pressed against her to simulate the birth process'. The idea was that Candace would be reborn to her adoptive mother. What happened, of course, was she died from asphyxiation.

I mention this because it is a good example of how adoption has become big business, and with big business come the leeches and flakes. I spent a day surfing adoption websites, visiting discussion forums and pages for prospective adoptive parents to advertise their credentials.

Most surreal was a site run by a private adoption company where you could choose between Chinese, Vietnamese, Indian and other nationalities of children like browsing an online restaurant guide. I discovered there is even an *Adoption for Dummies* book to go with *Windows XP for Dummies, Migraines for Dummies* and *Gifts from the Kitchen for Dummies.*

After eight hours of staring at a computer screen, the word *adoption* began to blur into the word *abortion.* Although they are opposites in obvious ways, they are both better than the third alternative, which is to be alive and unwanted. And that applies to Vietnamese babies as much as to English ones. Dickens, himself an adoptee, was clearly outraged at the treatment of unwanted children in Victorian Britain. But for a contemporary adoptee like me, with loving parents and a regretful birth mother, it is easy to forget that fate has indeed been kind to me.

I once heard a welfare spokeswoman state, as if it were an incontrovertible truth, that it was every child's right to be loved. Surely for the word "right" to have any meaning it must be attainable as well as deserved, and with so many neglected children in Britain alone how can this be feasible? The truth must be that a child is lucky if they are loved because if they aren't there is not much they can do about it. No child with loving adoptive parents wants to grow up feeling grateful for receiving what another child takes as their right, but looking back on their childhood from an objective standpoint the only reasonable response is gratitude.

My internet research actually made me glad to have been adopted in a more conservative era. It may have been secretive back then, but at least it wasn't a blatant commercial transaction. The current cost for two Americans to adopt a Vietnamese child, including airfare and accommodation while over there, is more than $20,000.

There is also something about these modern "open adoptions" – where birth mother and child never lose touch – that worries me. I wouldn't want my adoptive parents to be that laid-back. Jealousy may be politically incorrect, but it is real. Today's adoptive parents have a fine line to tread. If they encourage too much openness between their child and the birth mother, the child may end up thinking that he belongs to neither of them and that he may even be returned to a birth parent if circumstances change. If, on the other hand, they are too secretive about their child's biological past, the child may grow up thinking he has something to be ashamed of.

I can feel myself getting carried away: I almost want to say I'm *glad* I'm adopted. In truth, being adopted has so defined who I am that I can't imagine what it must be like to be "biological". The idea seems no less farfetched than being female or French. One positive thing I can say, however, is I don't feel like a victim anymore. When I start playing the wounded adoptee, I get a sick feeling and want to stop. I'm not going to pretend I love myself all the time, but I don't think I'm any more *wrong* as a person than anyone else. Of course, Steve Decker is still godlike but I must like it that way.

It seems extremely unlikely that I will U-turn into a raging alcoholic or sex fiend. More likely, I will continue the long slide into becoming a boring old man set in his ways, which is a success story of a kind, a heading towards Freud's desired state of 'common unhappiness'. My wife, of course, may have a different opinion on that.

* * *

I'm now a firm believer in the doubling rule. An everyday incident of a mother shouting at her son to stop treating the place like a hotel became, for me, an attack on my place in the family. It wasn't that I told myself: *I'm being treated like this because I'm adopted.* I knew I was adopted, which made me feel insecure, which in turn made an everyday attack feel personal. Seen through this hyper-vigilance, every criticism or perceived abandonment had the potential to be doubled.

I wonder if someone abused as a child or growing up gay, physically disabled or even in a war zone, in fact anyone growing up feeling marginalised, might also experience the doubling rule.

I was, and still can be, motivated by a desire to blame and punish. Alison wasn't there when I was growing up and anyway she wasn't the one in charge, my parents were. It followed it must be their fault if I felt I didn't fit in. So I self-sabotaged in order to remain a victim, which had the dual benefit of insulating me from rejection, as well as ensuring I remained a thorn in my parents' side – a living, livid accusation.

But of what was I accusing my parents?

In the first draft of this memoir, written a few years earlier, I listed here three ways in which I believed my parents had treated me differently from Rachel. I wrote that my parents – even if they wouldn't admit it to themselves – had felt that I was luckier to have them than they were to have me. This was why they'd seemed more interested in me *as a son*, than *as a person*.

I would always remember a conversation I had with the father of Neil Telfer (whom Will and I had briefly shared a study with at Cranford) during a Sunday pub lunch that Neil had invited me to with his parents. Mr Telfer had asked me what I thought about everything from Margaret Thatcher to the origin of the Aids virus, which had been hitting the headlines as a "gay plague" at the time. I'd been at first wary, then moved by the genuine interest he'd shown in what I had to say. Mr Telfer had clearly wanted to get to know me as a person. (Missing from this example is a vital piece of evidence: it was the first time we'd met. I doubt he maintained that level of interest in Neil over seventeen years – what son would want that? Comparing my parents' interest in me to a one-off evening was hardly fair.)

I wrote that the second way I'd been treated differently was that my parents had secretly resented me once Rachel was born, because they realised they could have had a family of their own after all. Now they had to deal with all the complicated, ambivalent feelings that came with having a "mixed" family, one with both adopted and biological children.

And I wrote, lastly, that they had played off nature against nurture, using genes to distance themselves from my shortcomings, while citing upbringing as the reason for my successes.

But when it came to writing the second draft, I knew the list didn't square with the two people I was "accusing". Mummy and Dad hadn't given me back to the adoption association once Mummy knew she was pregnant with Rachel, because they'd loved me too much even to consider it. The truth was that Rachel and I had been treated as equally as two siblings of different sex could be. In short, there was no objective evidence to support any of the three accusations.

Why, then, had I felt their validity for most of my life, and intensely so in my twenties? Each accusation *could* be true. Each could be supported by examples, even if Simon could argue the examples had been taken out of context. Why would I make up such things? Surely it would have been easier and made more sense to have flung my arms around my parents and thanked them for loving me as their own son?

Then it dawned on me: I thought the accusations were true. And therefore they were – in the world I'd created for myself, which is the only place any of us lives in.

I decided to speak to my mother about my adoption and see how this revelation sat with her replies. We'd never really gone through the whole story of my adoption in one go, so it was an overdue conversation anyway.

I went around for supper one evening when I was sure Dad would be out at one of his rugby club meetings. I felt sure that if I got them together, they'd only go so far before retreating behind family values slogans.

We were nibbling from the cheese board when I mentioned that I'd been reading a book about adoption by a clinical psychologist. I decided not to mention that the book was entitled *The Primal Wound: Understanding the adopted child* (too loaded in favour of the adoptee's misery); or that the author hailed from America (crucible of all things wacko, in my mother's opinion). Instead I said that the author was an adoptive mother, so the book hadn't been written by one of those psychologists who made money out of blaming the parents. The book's author clearly appreciated all sides of the adoption "triangle", which, I explained, referred to the child, adoptive mother and – leave her to last – birth mother.

Mummy said she'd like to read it, which I took to be a good start.

I nudged the conversation on: 'You know the time I didn't say anything or make a sound for a whole month, and you had to call a doctor?'

'Ye-es,' Mummy said, waiting.

'Do you think I could have been protesting at being separated from Alison?'

Mummy laughed – with genuine relief, I think. 'Don't be daft! It was after you'd had your tonsils out.'

Bang went my theory about when my "primal wound" had kicked in. I asked Mummy if I'd been withdrawn in any way after I'd arrived from the adoption association.

Mummy replied that I'd been hungry and boisterous. 'And you didn't let up for the next ten years!' She added that there had been nothing untoward in my behaviour in any way throughout my childhood.

No protracted silences or alarming screaming fits, no illnesses that could be psychosomatic?

None, my mother said. I seemed perfectly normal and content. Up to my mid-twenties, when I withdrew. Why I changed then, she didn't know, although she suspected it had something to do with that therapist I'd been recommended by her osteopath. She would never forgive that woman for suggesting I'd been given away twice, once by Alison and a second time when I was sent to prep school.

I decided against telling Mummy that it was her osteopath who'd told me that; I wanted to keep the focus on what mattered.

As we went over her memories of the process of adopting and then getting to know me, I could see both of us thinking the same thing: *she and Dad had done everything they could to give me a happy and fulfilled childhood.*

There was one aspect of adoption, however, about which a confluence of opinion seemed unlikely. Mummy refused even to countenance the idea that I could have arrived from the adoption association already in anguish as a result of being separated from my birth mother. The whole promise of adoption, of taking a newborn baby and treating it as if it were yours, was compromised by such a suggestion.

I saw the familiar mixture of sadness and irritation in Mummy's eyes when she realised that I *did* countenance such an idea. To Mummy, it was another example of how I'd let interfering therapists plant ideas in my head. She said it was fanciful to imagine that a person could remember what had happened to them when they were ten days old.

The obvious thing to ask Mummy next was if she believed at all in the idea of an unconscious part of the mind. I could imagine how the discussion would go: I would try to stay calm, as Mummy said of course she believed in the "subconscious" in terms of intuition. What she found deplorable was when therapists helped people "retrieve" often completely fabricated memories from their childhood, especially when these so-called memories were then used as evidence in court.

I wanted to keep the conversation on us, so I tried to draw Mummy in by admitting that I was by no means certain of the existence of a "primal wound". I said that the reason why I thought it might exist, however, was because it was the only way to explain how I felt. I told her that growing up knowing I'd been rejected by my birth mother had obviously affected my self-esteem, but it didn't seem enough to explain the traumatic effect that being adopted had had on me.

Mummy agreed without skipping a beat, which surprised me. I'd have imagined that she would have regarded anything with the word "traumatic" in it as attention-seeking. Perhaps her visit to The Lodge had made her view me in a different light. And once the existence of trauma had been conceded, it was infinitely preferable for it to have been caused by the adoption process than by upbringing.

I told Mummy that I had always felt like a fraud, a pretend person.

'We're all frauds to some extent,' Mummy said, surprising me again, this time by her frankness.

'I agree,' I said. 'But for me, feeling like a pretend person comes *before* feeling like a real person. It's my first feeling, my position of rest.'

Careful, I thought. This is a Big Conversation. Don't say anything for effect. Remember, some things cannot be unsaid.

But I felt I still hadn't made myself clear. 'It's really an underlying dread. That's the nearest I can get to describing what the primal wound feels like, if indeed that's what it is.'

'A dread of what?'

'Of – being found out. And then given away again. I think in fact it's about feeling powerless.' I could see my mother bristling at the phrase *given away again*, and immediately clarified, 'Of course, I never for one moment thought you'd do that – give me away. But the feeling that life was arbitrary, that things happened *to you*, has been with me for as long as I can remember. It's in my *body*. That's what makes me think it could go back to a primal wound, rather than just be the result of growing up *knowing* I was adopted.'

I knew this was why I'd always felt a guardedness when Mummy and I hugged. But I decided this would be too hurtful for Mummy to hear. Now, I think I missed a chance to show her empathy. Mummy must have felt that slight holding back, and it must have been awful for her. You only have to watch the childlike pain on a parent's face when their baby *by birth* ignores them, or runs off with the other parent, to imagine how much worse it has to be for an adoptive parent. Especially an adoptive mother, who must be yearning for the unique mother–child bond.

At some point Mummy got up to make coffee. I can see her coming through the kitchen arch with two cups, asking me if I thought they'd done the right thing telling me I was adopted so young.

I replied that I thought they did the only thing they could have done, which was follow the advice they were given by the experts. I told her I'd met a number of adopted people who were told, or found out, when they were teenagers. One who found out from his mother's will. And the resentment they felt against their parents for deceiving them was palpable. I said that, in the end, I thought it came down to how you wanted your adoption issues served up. The younger you were the more bewildered you felt, the older you were the more betrayed.

In response to Mummy's quizzical look, I said I'd met these other adoptees at NORCAP meetings, the National

Organisation for the Counselling of Adoptees and Parents. I explained that there were meetings once a month in smoke-filled rooms in cities around Britain.

Mummy nodded, taking it in. Again, she'd surprised me. I'd expected her to be dismissive of such "navel-gazing", but if anything she seemed impressed by my attending such a group. Perhaps she felt it added authority to what I was saying.

I realised that the most amazing thing about this conversation was that we were having it in the way we were. We were two adults, listening to each other.

And I could see that Mummy felt a lot now, and had felt a lot then. She was not dismissing it all as a figment of my imagination. She'd wrestled with how best to deal with Rachel's arrival; she'd worried about sending me away to boarding school so young. I could say, in wonderful hindsight, that I thought Dad and she had made some wrong decisions, but I couldn't accuse them of not caring.

I find it interesting that one of the first things I am asked when I tell someone I am adopted (which I don't do very often) is if I resemble Alison in any ways.

'I have her eyes,' I say.

'And personality?'

'We are both passionate, some might say gushing. I think we share a childlike quality.'

But soon I am compelled to counter the genes argument with evidence of the importance of a child's environment, by adding that apparently strangers would come up to me as a young boy and coo, 'Doesn't he look like his father!' As for being passionate, I have never met anyone with more passion about something than my dad has for rugby. He makes Patrick Moore seem bored by the sky at night in comparison.

And then there is the third point in the personality triangle to consider: the possibility that a person is born with a unique personality irrespective of genes or environment. After all, I know identical twins whose parents swear they had distinct personalities almost from birth. Maybe I would have been a gushing and childlike yak herder if my parents had been Tibetan. From my tone, it is probably evident that I find this particular discussion rather circular. I suppose the reason why people latch onto it is because it's such an obvious talking point.

The focus of this memoir is almost entirely on environment, because it provides so much material to work on, but also because the part played by genes or God in forming personality seems to be purely a matter of conjecture. No doubt I am also firmly in the environment camp because it can be examined, prodded and theorised about, giving me a sense of control over my life.

The real cliff-hanger in this story is not, after all, at the end of Chapter 2, when I'm unsure if I'll meet Alison again. The real cliff-hanger is being left to wonder what happens when, and if, I have children of my own. Only once I've felt the sting of their analysis of my parenting will this story be finished. I await my oldest child's memoirs with trepidation.

But finish, albeit early, I must. Or I'll be like that Lodge veteran who walked around the perimeter in his US Navy baseball cap, forever working on his "trauma bonds". How to finish, then?

I started with a string of coincidences, so I'll end with one. Don McCleod's wife, Sue, enrols on a painting class in London. Her teacher is called Lorna Prowse, using her maiden name since her divorce. When Lorna tells Sue that she does most of her painting in Cornwall, the surname and location fall into place. 'Do you have a sister called Alison?' Sue asks her teacher.

Lorna, already an expert in coincidences, replies that she does.

And now I can go back to writing fiction, where life is so much more believable.

Note

While writing *Special & Odd* I decided to investigate how my experience of adoption fits into the bigger picture. On the sociological impact of adoption, I found US psychologist David Brodzinsky's report 'Long-term outcomes in adoption' (published in *The Future of Children*, *Vol.3*, pp. 153-66, 1993) to contain much relevant research; and on the psychological implications, *The Primal Wound* by clinical psychologist Nancy Verrier (Boston: Gateway Press, 1993) is captivating in the clarity of her analysis. I came across the terrible, cautionary story of the death of a young adopted girl in the care of two attachment therapists, in a 2001 article in the US newspaper *The Rocky Mountain News*. Finally, I found Robert Bly's *Iron John* (London: Ebury Press, 2001) to contain many interesting thoughts about gender roles in our time.